15-

15-

THE ART OF
BRONZE
BRASS
AND
COPPER

THE ART OF
BRONZE
BRASS
AND
COPPER

Exquisite artefacts
from ancient times
to the 20th century

JAN DIVIŠ

Editor of the English Edition: Peter Hornsby

HAMLYN

Text by Jan Diviš
Translated by Till Gottheinerová
Photographs from Czechoslovak collections by
Soňa Divišová
Drawings by Ivan Kafka
Graphic design by František Prokeš

Designed and produced by Aventinum
English language edition first published 1991
by The Hamlyn Publishing Group Limited,
a division of Reed International Books Limited,
Michelin House, 81 Fulham Road,
London SW3 6RB

ISBN 0 600 57268 4

Printed in Czechoslovakia by Polygrafia, Prague
2/09/09/51-01

Contents

Foreword

This book is intended for readers who are interested in objects made of copper and its alloys, bronze and brass. The publication of this book reflects the growing interest in this field and the increasing number of collectors, who appreciate the beauty of this, at first sight commonplace material and the skill of the craftsmen who gave it shape.

The greater part of the book deals with Europe; diversions to territories outside Europe were necessary only in discussing the beginning of the production of copper and its alloys. If the book is to fulfil what it sets out to do it needs to acquaint the reader with the use of this metal in the history of art and sum up all that is known about it. It is assumed that the reader has little previous knowledge of the subject, and therefore the development of the technology and the object is given in broad cultural context. In addition, a special chapter deals in outline with the production of copper and its alloys in the past so that the reader might become acquainted with the technology used in this field. These chapters are meant for the collector — especially the beginner in the field. An appendix to the book contains a glossary that provides brief information on the basic terms, which collectors are likely to encounter. Special attention has been paid to terms describing ornamental motifs and to various alloys based on copper, especially those that are found only in highly specialized publications.

Because more is known and because many objects survive, stress has been placed on the eighteenth and nineteenth centuries. The other periods are dealt with to show the reader the continuity of development and the main trends of each period. The illustrations, both photographs and drawings, were selected with this in mind to give the reader a picture of the main types of objects and their decoration.

Readers who have no specialist knowledge of history will appreciate that the names of countries or regions are mostly given in terms used today in preference to the ancient names.

The book will, I trust, fulfil what it sets out to do if, besides providing information, it wins new admirers for the beautiful materials, copper, brass and bronze.

In conclusion, I would like to express my gratitude to the Museum of Decorative Arts in Prague, the National Museum in Prague, the Museum of the City of Prague, and all parish authorities in Bohemia and Slovakia who granted permission to study and photograph objects belonging to them.

Jan Diviš

Introduction

Copper was the first metal that Man learnt to work and use. This metal, in its pure form or as various alloys, was and remains important for mankind.

It is clear that the use of copper did not only come about because it was soft and pliable when cold and could thus be easily worked. Another reason for its use was that, apart from gold, it is a metal that appears most often in nature in pure form, though it is not always completely pure. The ancient Greeks attributed the discovery of the art of working copper to Cadmus. During his travels he is said to have found copper on the second largest Greek island of Euboea (today known as Evvoia) near the town of Chalcis. From it the Greeks derived their name for copper 'chalkos'. The Bible, on the other hand, attributes this discovery to Tubalcain, the son of Cain (Genesis 4.22). All these legendary reports confirm that the ancient nations were aware of the importance and significance of this metal for human society.

Pure copper was found in quantities too small to satisfy demand, and soon it began to be won from a variety of ores. This was first achieved in Anatolia in about the seventh millennium B.C. The Egyptians were mining copper in the mountainous Sinai Peninsula by the fourth millennium B.C. The best known Greek copper ore mines, apart from Euboea, were on Delos, a mountainous little island in the Cyclads. Cyprus, too, had important copper mines, and from there the Latin term for copper 'cuprum' was derived. The mining of copper, gold and silver ensured the inhabitants of Cyprus a relatively high standard of living in ancient times. The richest copper ore deposits in Antiquity were those in Hispania, present-day Spain, from where the Phoenician merchants exported it from the port of Tartessus to all regions surrounding the Mediterranean. The most important copper ore deposits for central and northern Europe lay in the Alps and the Tatras in present-day Slovakia.

The Greeks learnt the skill of mining ores, and this included copper ore, from the Phoenicians, who were the first to open up mines along the coast and on the islands of the Mediterranean Sea. Work in the surface mines was similar to work in quarries. To mine ore deep in the ground they either sank shafts or cut horizontal drifts which branched out into narrower tunnels along the veins of ore. In the Greek mines these shafts were rectangular while in Roman mines they were either circular or eliptical. In southern Attica, Greece, some two thousand such shafts survive from the beginning of history when silver and lead were mined there. The average depth of the shafts ranges from 25 to 50 metres and some have been found reaching to a depth of 150 metres. The side tunnels, the places where the actual mining took place, were often no higher than one metre so that the miner was forced to work lying down. The rocks or ores were taken from the mines on barrows, or were transported to the surface in baskets or leather bags using simple machinery. To light up the tunnels the miner used little lamps filled with oil, which they attached to their foreheads. These helped to detect the presence of poisonous gases in the mines.

The Romans were highly successful in mining ores. They did so by sending a large labour force to the mines. Slaves and convicts were employed but paid labour from various strata of the free or semi-free provincial population was also used. This work-force included women and children. The Romans were aware of the strategic and economic importance of mines and therefore established military camps in the vicinity to protect the mine territory and to keep order in the mines.

We do not possess any reports on how ores were mined in barbarian territory, but there cannot have been great differences between mining by the Romans and mining north of the Alps. The basic mining tools will have been identical: hammer, mallet, chisel, pickaxe, hoe and shovel. The rocks were broken up with a hammer, wedges and crowbar or a fire was lit along the wall and the rock split in the heat. They also used dry wooden wedges which they punched into the rocks. When soused with water, these would swell and break the rocks up into smaller pieces.

An important element for the production of bronze was tin. In the Mycenaean era the Phoenicians imported to the Mediterranean region large quantities of tin from Britain, and for that reason the British Isles were called Kassiterides (Tin Isles) by the Greeks. Most of the mining took place in and around Cornubia, today's Cornwall. Later, deposits were discovered in Spain. Some scholars link the Greek word 'kassiteros' with the Sanscrit word for tin 'kastira' and believe that, in the earliest days, the Phoenician merchants also brought tin from India.

The qualities of copper which make it easy to work, highly ductile and resistant to climatic influences, determine its place in the production of vessels, sculptures and weapons. These qualities also set limits on its use. The ancient miners soon found, perhaps through working ores containing foreign matter, that copper alloyed with tin possessed highly advantageous qualities, and so they began to make this alloy deliberately. Today we call it **bronze**. It is thought that this im-

Table of composition of various historical bronze objects:

Object:	copper	tin	zinc	lead	iron	silver	nickel	other
Epyptian sculpture	58.6	5.2	22.0	5.1	8.8	—	—	—
Mycenaean sword	86.4	13.0	—	0.11	0.17	—	0.15	—
Greek bronze from Corfu	81.5	18.1	—	—	—	—	—	—
Greek bronze from Cyprus	97.2	vestiges	—	0.1	1.3	—	—	1.3 arsenic 0.3 gold
Roman mirror	63.4	19.0	—	17.3	—	—	—	—
Roman sculpture	80.8	9.4	1.9	7.7	—	—	—	—
Prehistoric bronze from Bohemia	79.6	9.3	—	7.7	2.9	—	—	—
Prehistoric sword (La Tène)	91.5	6.7	—	0.4	0.2	—	0.24	—
Persian cannon (1677)	86.1	4.6	—	9.1	—	—	—	0.1 arsenic
Louis XIV (Keller, 1699)	91.4	1.7	5.5	1.4	—	—	—	—
Cannon barrel (19th century)	90.0	10.0	—	—	—	—	—	—

portant discovery was made in Mesopotamia in about 3000 to 2800 B.C., but it may have occurred in Egypt and in India.

Europe became acquainted with bronze about a thousand years later. Bronze is an alloy of copper with two or more compounds, mainly tin. The preparation of bronze and its casting is easier than that of iron. The chief qualities of good bronze include the fine structure of the alloy, great compactness and hardness, easy fusibility and good qualities in casting. It is worked on a lathe and filed more easily than even copper, and it has a pleasant reddish-gold to gold colour. With the passing of time bronze acquires a patina, a beautiful dark green coating due to atmospheric effects.

Present-day bronze metallurgy shows many bronzes of different qualities, and they are used mainly for technological purposes. The ancient division of bronzes was based on the tin content in the alloy. They distinguished the main types: bell bronze contained 20—25 per cent of tin, gun metal 10 per cent of tin, mirror bronze 30 per cent of tin and coin bronze 1—3 per cent of tin. An alloy for copper and tin at the ratio of 10 : 1 is regarded as classical bronze.

Bronze-makers soon found that by the addition of a small portion of other metals they could improve some of the qualities of bronze. By adding 1—3 per cent of lead, bronze could be more easily repaired and polished. Zinc made casting easier, the alloy was free of bubbles and could be chased better. When the advantages of these alloys were known, the required portion of zinc was added by means of calamine. Chemical analysis of ancient bronzes shows traces of arsenic, iron and nickel, but the amounts present suggest that they were probably not added to the alloy intentionally but were associated with ore of the other elements (see table). Corinthian bronzes were particularly valued by ancient civilisations for their alleged content of precious metals. Modern sculptors use alloys of copper, tin, zinc and lead. Bronze works of art, at present, are usually made of an alloy composed of 80—90 per cent of copper, 3—8 per cent of tin, 1—10 per cent of zinc and 1—3 per cent of lead.

Another important alloy is **brass.** It is an alloy of copper and zinc, sometimes with the addition of a small quantity of other metals such as lead, tin, nickel or iron. According to its use, the ratio of the individual metals in the alloy varies. Brass with a large copper content is harder, more ductile, more malleable, can be well cast and has good atmospheric resistance. The addition of lead improves the quality of brass for machine turning but reduces its ductility.

The possibility of changing the qualities of alloys by changing the ratio of copper to zinc gave rise to a larger number of different kinds of brass. For example, red brass contains 9—19 per cent of zinc and 91—81 per cent of copper. It is very ductile, can easily be hammered cold, and melted it is very tenuous and can therefore be well cast. Yellow brass is an alloy of 68—70 per cent of copper and 32—30 per cent of zinc. It is rather fragile, not malleable but can be well rolled. White brass contains 15—42 per cent of copper, and the rest is zinc. It is very brittle and is suitable only for casting.

In the seventeenth century objects made their appearance in Europe coming from what was then Siam, now Thailand, and they became known by the Malay term of **tambago** (tombac). Tambago is a soft brass containing such a small percentage of zinc that it is red to golden yellow in colour. Some consider an alloy with less than 18 per cent of zinc to be tambago, others place the border between brass and tambago at 25 per cent of zinc in the alloy. Alloys with a high zinc content are sometimes called semi-tambago. Some producers today using the good qualities of tambago for gilding or minting coins, medals, badges and bijouterie give their products various trade names such as Simili-or, Chrysocal, Oreide, Prince's metal, Bristol brass, Monel metal, etc.

Another type of brass alloy is **paktong**, which is the Chinese name for white copper. Paktong is a nickel brass, i.e. an alloy of copper, zinc and nickel at ratios varying from producer to producer. Nickel quickly removes the colour of the brass so that, with a 10 per cent nickel content in the alloy it becomes quite white. Paktong is an alloy of copper, nickel and zinc, which varies considerably in its actual composition. Objects of paktong were brought from China and put on the European market in the course of the eighteenth century and soon became very popular for their bright colour, high and relatively easy polish and, by no means least, for the good mechanical qualities and resistance to chemical influences.

According to recent research, it seems that the centre of brass production is likely to have been the Near East, probably Palestine, where some time around 1300 B.C. the first alloy of copper and zinc was produced. The production and use of bronze and brass is evident at a very early date. The artistic and technical use of the two alloys is similar and for that reason they were not strictly distinguished in ancient times. In the Middle Ages they used bronze and brass to make baptismal fonts, tombstones, candlesticks, inkwells, and various bowls. In the case of great works of art, where we would now use bronze, they sometimes used brass, for example, Peter Vischer's Sebald tombstone in Nuremberg. The strict dividing line between the two alloys was laid down in the sixteenth century when the newly rediscovered classical bronzes of Antiquity were again valued for the quality of the bronze alloy and the beauty of their patina. The very term 'bronze' for an alloy of copper and tin appeared at that time. It was probably first used and explained by the author of the oldest comprehensive work on metallurgy, the Italian Vannuccio Biringuccio, in his work *De la pirotechnia libri X.*

The Prehistoric Period

Nowadays, the range of different metals and their alloys which serve our civilization is regarded as a matter of course. We give little thought to the arduous road that had to be followed to reach our present-day cultural and technical level. Even though little is known about the prehistoric period we can distinguish with fair precision the main stages of the development of human society, thanks to the diligence of generations of scholars.

Prehistoric Man lived in small tribes and initially they lived by hunting animals and collecting fruits. The tools and weapons that they needed to keep alive or to defend themselves were fashioned from the materials at hand — wood, bones and stones, especially carefully fashioned flint. It is likely that it was in the eighth millennium B.C. that an important breakthrough occurred in the history of Mankind. Man began to concentrate on plants for his food while hunting began, by slow stages, to lose some of its importance. In brief, Man began to live by agriculture and by pasturing. The long period in the history of Mankind, which we are accustomed to call the Stone Age, after the material used for the production of work and hunting tools, ended in Europe at the beginning of

1 The Khasemhemwy copper vessel with a riveted double spout. Egypt, 2nd Dynasty. University of Pennsylvania, Philadelphia.

11

Bronze mirror with handle in the shape of a female figure. Egypt, New Kingdom.

the second millennium B.C., when the first bearers of the oldest Bronze Age cultures began to penetrate to the Continent. This basic change of material used for utensils and tools, i.e. from stone to metal, was not a European discovery. Once again, as several times before, the civilizations of the eastern Mediterranean proved their superiority.

If we go back in search of the use of copper, the basis of bronze alloys, it seems that the first traces of copper can be detected in the seventh millennium B.C. in inland Asia Minor.

The Egyptians mined copper from *c.* 5000 to 4500 B.C. The inhabitants of Mesopotamia used copper ore at the end of the fourth century B.C. In the eastern Mediterranean region, and in southeastern Europe, the local population worked copper mines from the third millennium B.C. and in *c.* 2500—2000 B.C. this knowledge spread to Central and Western Europe. This period, during which the first objects of copper, mainly working tools, appeared, is known as the chalkolit.

The time when people learnt to work metals varied greatly. This can be shown through the 'copper culture' in North America found in the territory of present-day Minnesota, Wisconsin, parts of Michigan, Iowa and Ontario. The objects and weapons of this culture were wrought almost exclusively of copper. Most of the finds are spear points, from which one may deduce that the bearers of this culture were hunters. This 'copper culture' flourished on the North American continent in the seventh century A.D.

The discovery of an alloy of copper and

tin, i.e. bronze, meant a revolution in human society. Yet we cannot definitively say where it took place nor append a precise date. Generally it can be said that in the period around 2900 B.C. bronze was already known in the Near East, in Egypt, Mesopotamia and also in India. It seems highly likely that the invention took place when the people were forced to work copper ore metallurgically, since the finds of pure natural copper no longer sufficed to cover their needs, and the impurity in the ore encouraged experiments in alloying copper.

The high standard of culture and art of Egypt is generally appreciated. Egyptian art left its mark on the art of the neighbouring countries and regions where attention was chiefly paid to architecture and sculpture. The crafts are somewhat overshadowed as they involved ordinary materials, including bronze and copper. This may be due to the fact that the Egyptian goldsmiths produced such fine work. Yet even the products of ordinary metals were of high quality, even though iron was known in Egypt by the third millennium B.C., it was not used to any great extent until the Hellenistic and Roman period. At the beginning they worked copper, which they obtained from deposits in the Arabian desert. Copper vessels have been found that show excellent craftsmanship, and they can be dated to the period of the Old Kingdom, the First and Second Dynasties (3000—2778 B.C.). Objects of bronze appeared later. Tin needed for the production of bronze was imported from Asia. Bronze was used more widely in the New Kingdom, from 1580 B.C. onwards. Utensils of various kind were made — bowls to hold liquids, metal furniture ornaments, heating devices, torch-holders or objects for toilet use, such as pincers to pluck out hairs and mirrors with figural handles.

The second region of interest to us is that part of Asia which we call the Near East and Asia Minor. Various states and nations alternated fairly rapidly there so that conditions under which art and the crafts might flourish were not as favourable as in Egypt. Nonetheless, some outstanding works were produced which are proof of the high level of the craftsmen of the time. The oldest objects are the work of Sumerian metal-casters. The Sumerians came to Mesopotamia in the middle

Bronze axe used in the cult. Luristan.

2   Bronze weight in the shape of a reclining lion from the period 530—380 B.C. Found at Susa in Iran. Musée National du Louvre, Paris.

of the fourth millennium B.C., possibly from India or from Central Asia. In their new homeland this highly gifted people invented, among other things — wedge writing, a twelve-month calendar, the potter's wheel, waggons with wheels and the decimal system. They clearly knew how to work copper and bronze, proved by objects found at Larsa, Khafaji and al-Ubayd. The three bronze capricorns found at Larsa can be dated to the year 2000 B.C.

From prehistoric time, Anatolia was an important link between the advanced cultures of the Middle East and Egypt. Numerous finds by Turkish archeologists show that, from the early third millennium, there existed a flourishing culture, which attained a high level in working bronze. Cult objects have been excavated (a bronze square with 16 panels) as well as objects for daily use, such as a bridle with figural ornaments representing a horse tamer (now in the Louvre). These can be

dated to the nineteenth or eighteenth century B.C.

In the 1930s bronze objects appeared on the antiquities market, mainly horse curbs, generally of very high artistic standard. From the point of view of style it was impossible to attribute them to any known cultural sphere, especially when the Armenian middlemen did not want to reveal the origin of these objects. Since, at the beginning, most of the objects offered were horse curbs, some scholars assumed that these bronze objects came from Scythian tombs. Soon, however, objects other than horse curbs began to be offered, for example hair slides, shaft ornaments, small pots or ceremonial axes. It became clear that these objects did not originate in the Scythian region, and the interest of scholars turned to inland Iran. In 1938 Erich F. Schmidt undertook a trip to the region called Luristan in the Zagros Mountains. There, indeed, he found in a sanctuary the type of object

13

3 Two-part stone mould for casting bronze needles. Knovíz Culture, 12th—7th century B.C. Found near the village of Zvolinĕves in Bohemia. Length of the larger part 15.5 cm. National Museum, Prague.

that had appeared on the antiquities market. Since horse curbs are most typical of that culture, it was clear that the makers of these objects were, in the first place, horsemen and horse breeders. The curbs are richly ornamented, usually with two capricorns, wild goats or winged animals. Other objects are also of high artistic standard such as shaft ornaments, swords, daggers, ceremonial axes, votive needles in the shape of a disk with human face, ear-rings or bracelets and rings. The Luristan bronzes are usually dated to the years 1500—800 B.C. Even at a later period, Persia did not lose its cultural originality. Under the Achaemenian Dynasty (530—380 B.C.) interesting bronze ware was produced. Typical examples of the high level of Persian metal-casting are bronze weights in the shape of a reclining lion found at Susa and now in the Louvre in Paris. Even during the reign of the Parthian Dynasty (250 B.C.—A.D.226) art and the crafts maintained their high level, to judge by present research.

Let us now turn our attention to the Aegean region. There existed two main cultural centres: Crete and Mycenae. In the Late Stone Age people were already living on Crete, then a mountainous, thickly wooded island. The Bronze Age began on the island in the middle of the third millennium B.C. and lasted to the end of the second millennium. At that time, Cretan civilization reached its highest point and took its name from the mythical King Minos — Minoan culture. The knowledge of how to work metal meant, as in other regions, that there was a striking change in the quality of working tools and weapons and in the people's way of thinking. The production of metal objects involved the co-operation of a larger number of people than hitherto. This was reflected in the type of settlements, some of which evolved into townships. It has been estimated that, at the time when Crete flourished, fifty to eighty thousand people lived in the town of Knossos. With the spread of the crafts came the growth of trade.

Crete traded not only with Greece but had contacts with more distant lands, such as Italy, Sicily and Spain and, in an easterly direction, with Troy and other countries on the eastern shores of the Mediterranean Sea. This was not interrupted even by the unknown disaster that struck Crete

4 One half of a stone mould for casting bronze rings. Knovíz Culture,
12th—7th century B.C. Found near the village of Zvoliněves in Bohemia. Length
11 cm. National Museum, Prague.

in the second half of the eighteenth
century B.C., as evidenced by signs of
the destruction of buildings and palaces.
Apart from the famous Cretan pottery
and objects of precious metals, excavations have brought to light large numbers
of bronze objects, mainly weapons and
small statues. The latter were part of the
cult, since in their religious practices the
Cretans made sacrifices of living animals
and sacrificed pottery and bronze figures
of humans and animals. A rare find was
made in the palace at Mallia where
a craftsman's workshop was uncovered
with slate moulds for casting bronze chisels, engraving tools, double axes, scrapers
and even mirrors. In the Late Bronze
Age (1580—1100 B.C.) Cretan civilization
gradually declined. This enabled the
Greek tribes living on the Peloponnese to
undertake invasions of Crete and take
over the island. Cretan civilization in all
its branches left a strong mark on Greek
culture, art, music and religion.

The Mycenaean culture is that of the
mainland Greeks in the sixteenth to
twelfth century B.C., and takes its name
from the town of that name in the Argolis,
in the Peloponnese north of Argos. The
Mycenaean culture began to flourish in
the fourteenth century B.C. after the fall of
the Cretan palaces. At that time, Mycenaean ships began to sail over the entire
Mediterranean Sea. Bronze tools and im-
plements played a decisive role. In agriculture bronze sickles were used for the
harvest and the warriors carried bronze
weapons. The craftsmen produced jewellery and bronze vessels. Copper was probably imported from Cyprus since there
was an increase of Mycenaean pottery on
Cyprus from the fourteenth century B.C. It
is also known that the Mycenaeans imported tin ore from Britain in large quantities.

When architect Michael Ventris suc-
ceeded, in 1952, in deciphering the Cre-
tan-Mycenaean Linear B script, used in
the Mycenaean cultural sphere, he discovered that the texts on the tablets contained merely lists for commercial purposes. They did not hold any references to
historical events. At the end of the twelfth
century B.C. the Dorians invaded Greece
and probably settled in the mountainous
regions of the northwestern Balkan Peninsula. The Mycenaean towns were burnt
down, destroyed and abandoned. The tra-

Bronze funerary idol. Luristan.

dition of the Mycenaean culture of the Achaeans continued however in Greece, especially in craft techniques, religion and literature.

As has been shown the centre of the revolutionary discovery of how to work metals was the region along the eastern shores of the Mediterranean Sea. It is assumed that the knowledge of working copper and its alloys then passed from this highly developed cultural sphere to the European continent in two ways. One route led across the Iberian Peninsula, the other was via the Balkans. As proof of this hypothesis we have beautifully made daggers of flint in northern Europe, imitating the metal daggers of Central Europe. Similarly, on the British Isles, particularly the northern parts, Bronze Age culture did not flourish until the middle of the second millennium while in the more southerly parts of Europe Bronze Age culture had already established roots at the beginning of the second millennium. Central Europe, similarly, lagged behind the south. While the Neolithic period, the Late Stone Age, prevailed in Europe, in Egypt the culture of the Old Kingdom and in Mesopotamia that of the Sumerians reached great heights. In the Late Neolithic period, at the end of the third millennium B.C., there were striking changes in the various cultures, as excavations have shown. There are two groups to be considered: the people using stone war axes and those using bell-beakers. It is assumed that the people with the stone axes were the first Indo-Europeans in the Central European region. It is believed that individual groups of the Indo-European people began to scatter across the European continent at the time when copper was distinguished from bronze, i.e. some time at the end of the third millennium B.C. since, in the various Indo-European languages, the same term is used for metal, but each has a different name for copper. By the Iron Age, this scattered settlement of Indo-European peoples was completed.

The people with the stone war-axes were followed by the bell-beaker people. They came to Europe from the shores of North Africa via the Iberian Peninsula and already knew how to work copper. The bearers of the Bronze Age culture in the Early Bronze Age in Central Europe were the Straubin and Adlerberg Cul-

tures, the Únětice Culture and the Wessex Culture in the south of the British Isles, where they were influenced by the neighbouring Irish cultures with their bronze industry. Important for further development was the Urnifield Culture at the turn of the second to first millennium B.C., i.e. the Late Bronze Age and the beginning of the Early Iron Age. The people of the Urnfield Culture, who lived scattered over the entire territory stretching from the Carpathians to the British Isles and the Iberian Peninsula, are regarded by some scholars as the source that gave rise to the Celts.

It is interesting for a closer insight into the development and growth of the Bronze culture in Europe north of the Alps to identify where copper was mined in the earliest period. In the Late Stone Age, the Neolithic time, pure, natural copper was used to make some of the war axes, as modern physical analysis has shown. Far more important was the copper gained by smelting ore. This involves a profound knowledge of metallurgy, the building of kilns, making of moulds, methods of casting and, in the end, alloying copper with tin. New methods of work had to be evolved conditioned by the qualities of the new raw materials: forging, hammering, chasing, drawing of wires, etc. It is remarkable how, in the Early Bronze cultures of that part of Europe, there appeared objects that involved specialized methods and special materials for their production. One might cite, as an example, the production of bronze chains with closed links cast in one piece. To make such thin chains the prehistoric metal-caster must have used moulds of several parts, adapted to ensure that the last link cast was attached to the next to be cast.

There can be no doubt that the mastery of such technical knowledge and special metallurgical technology was already achieved in the Early Bronze Age, when there will have been specialized families of miners, metal-founders, metal-casters and metal-chisellers. We can assume that these crafts were the first to emerge from the sphere of home production and to become the domain of experienced specialist craftsmen. They would spread the knowledge of how to work metals throughout Europe.

The Europen Bronze culture was de-

16

5   A hoard of bronze daggers with
decorated blades. Únětice Culture, 19th to
15th century B.C. Found near the village of
Horoměřice in Bohemia. National Museum,
Prague.

6   Bronze cult wagonette. Milaveč Culture,
13th—10th century B.C. Found near the
village of Milaveč in Bohemia. Height of
cauldron 25 cm, length of wagonette 30 cm.
National Museum, Prague.

7 Bronze jug with spout. Etruscan export
to Central Europe, 5th century B.C. Found
near the village of Hradiště in Bohemia.
Height 23 cm. National Museum, Prague.

19

8   Bronze pail with handle
decorated with cast figures.
Central Italian export to
Central Europe, end of 1st
century B.C. Found near the
village of Dobřichov in
Bohemia.
National Museum, Prague.

9   Two bronze tripods. Italy, 1st century
A.D. Height 20.3 and 17.3 cm. Museum of
Decorative Arts, Prague.

10 Two bronze reliquary crosses of the type of crosses from the Holy Land. 11th century. Found in Prague. Height 6 and 8.5 cm. Museum of the City of Prague.

11   Two dishes of hammered copper
decorated with engraved part-figures of
angels. Maas region, 12th century. Diameter
23.5 and 27 cm. National Museum, Prague.

12   Two bronze censers. Bohemia, 13th
century. Height 17.5 and 12.5 cm. National
Museum, Prague.

13   Bronze cup found near the village of Libkovice in Bohemia. Silesian-Plátenice Culture, first half of 1st millennium B.C. Height 6.2 cm. National Museum, Prague.

pendent on deposits of metal ores. Natural pure copper appeared only so sporadically that it cannot have been adequate to meet their needs. It was assumed that the Alpine deposits were of great importance for mining ore in Central Europe. Scholars based their assumption on traces of prehistoric ore mining at Mittelberg and on the geographical location of finds of 'talents', copper raw material already used for trading. Modern methods of precision measuring of the mineralogical compounds of pure metal or alloys have brought a number of surprises. It was found that in the Early Bronze Age they already knew and used Carpathian copper — or rather deposits on the territory of present-day Slovakia. Other deposits will have been of similar importance and in the course of the second millennium these enabled the whole of Europe to turn to the production of bronze objects. There were also deposits in the Iberian Peninsula and in the British Isles. There were

areas where the production of copper and its alloys reached a high level, especially in the Danubian lowlands, the territories of present-day Spain, France and Germany as far as Scandinavia and to the east in the Volga river basin.

While local bronze culture flourished in the Danubian lowlands and at the foot of the Alps, a cultural centre arose in northern Italy, which began to influence its broad environs. Typical of such bronze vessels made in that area were situla. These were conical buckets, usually with a movable handle, with hammered strips of ornaments depicting scenes of life of northern Italy or showing various animal figures. In the sixth and fifth centuries B.C. they began to be exported to places north of the Alps. Situlas enjoyed popularity, and their import continued into the Hallstatt period and the early La Tène time. Busy trade contacts existed on a route from the Adriatic Sea to the Baltic region where the main article of trade was the

14 Two bronze pitchers
decorated with coral
incrustation, found at
Basse-Yutze near Metz in
France. La Tène period.
British Museum, London.

highly valued amber. This trade route is often called the Amber Route. In return for amber the people there acquired metal utensils.

This brings us to the time when the Celts were the dominant inhabitants in the regions from the Iberian Peninsula to the British Isles and from France to Central Europe, now Bohemia. In the fifth to first centuries B.C. they developed a culture, which we today call 'La Tène' after a locality in the shallows of Lake Neuenburg in Switzerland. The Celts are of exceptional importance for European culture. By the peak of the 'La Tène' period Celtic workshops had mastered the basic production processes and technology and

thus formed the base on which further centuries could draw. The Celts knew about advanced tanning techniques and the production of high quality materials so that, for instance, Hannibal's soldiers when crossing the Alps were supplied with material from Celtic workshops from the territory which is present-day France. Records inform us of the work of coppers and carpenters and of potters using the potter's wheel. The skills of metal-casting and chiselling were brought to perfection by the Celts. In founding techniques they knew in detail all the qualities of the various alloys and increasingly used the lost wax casting method. In the later 'La Tène' period, enamelling became widespread.

26

Enamel ornaments were used on luxury objects, on things of everyday use and on military shields. The Celts did not work only bronze. The importance of Celtic culture rests on their mastering the complex technique of mining and working iron and making it to such a degree of perfection that it could replace bronze for working tools, scythes, saws, drills and ploughshares. The far-reaching Celtic trade contacts and conquests showed in the products of Celtic craftsmen, who adopted designs from Greece and Italy. Celtic art was, in fact, a decorative art, where the motifs of Antiquity were given a Celtic spirit. The early style of these articles of craftsmanship preferred a flat system of decoration, which, from the third century B.C., changed into a three dimensional or a plastic style. Articles of excellent quality found in the British Isles and dating from the first century A.D. represent Celtic art at a later stage.

After the middle of the last century B.C. the Celts were surrounded on two sides by dangerous opponents. From the south, the Roman legions constantly moved the borders of Roman Empire further to the north, in the north the Germanic tribes were beginning their attacks. In the end, the Celts succumbed to these pressures. The importance of the Celts for European civilization was so great that the nations of Europe continued to draw on their heritage for many centuries.

Antiquity

It has already been said that metal working first occurred in the Near East and Asia Minor. The Early Bronze Age in Greek history was influenced by this development. The advantageous location on the coast enabled the inhabitants of Greece to make easy contact with neighbouring peoples in Asia Minor or on Crete, while the mainland was in those days more of an obstacle to trade and cultural contacts.

Revolutionary changes took place in Greece in the Middle Bronze Age (2000–1600 or 1550 B.C.). It is thought that, at that period, the original population from Asia Minor living in Greece was ousted from the country by new ethnic elements, probably Indo-Europeans and perhaps Greeks, and in this process most of the settlements of the Early Bronze Age were destroyed with the population declining dramatically. The newcomers bore the Middle Bronze Age culture and despite the disasters that accompanied these shifts they represented an advance in the progress of civilization. The horse was tamed and used as a draught animal and, from the thirteenth century B.C. on, even for riding. Pottery was for the first time shaped on the potter's wheel and, most importantly, those people worked in bronze.

We usually call the Late Bronze culture in Greece (1600 or 1550 to 1100 B.C.) the Mycenaean culture, discussed in the previous chapter. It should be said in addition that, after the invasion by the Greek tribe of the Dorians, the Aeolians, Ionians and Achaeans had to take refuge beyond the seas. The Achaeans occupied Crete and Cyprus, the Ionians the centre and the Aeolians the northwestern shores of Asia Minor. It is not surprising that these tempestuous events put an end to the advanced Mycenaean culture. The period that followed from the twelfth to the ninth century B.C. is usually known as the Dark Age. A period of decline about which very little is known.

From the eighth century the economy of Greece began to flourish thanks to slave labour, and this ultimately led to the establishment of the Greek city states. In the overall economic and cultural growth the use of toreutics or chased curved or embossed metal developed, especially the production of wrought metal vessels and military helmets. The city of Corinth achieved great fame with its bronze products. The vessels are often decorated with figural or ornamental friezes, mostly in relief with human heads, plant ornaments or animal bodies. These bronze vessels were of different sizes. A find in France provides proof of the achievement that Greek toreutics attained. At Vix near

Ornamental motifs on bronze objects from the La Tène period.

a Greek crater, or wine vessel, 164 cm high, 127 cm in diameter and weighing 208.6 kg. Such a crater would hold 1,100 litres of liquid. On the neck was a relief frieze, on which foot soldiers alternate with cavalrymen on a two-wheeled chariot drawn by four horses. Two mighty spiral-shaped handles ended at the lower end in a grinning Gorgon mask or face. On the lid of the vessel are relief figures of a smiling woman, perhaps the goddess Artemis. The tomb contained many objects of Etruscan origin including two flat dishes and a beak-shaped jug. The 'crater' itself is definitely of Greek origin and dates from the end of the sixth century B.C. Most scholars are of the opinion that it came from southern Italy in the vicinity of Toronto but some believe that this is actually Corinthian work.

Several conclusions can be drawn from this surprising find at Vix. In the first place, it provides proof that the wealth and assets of the Celtic rulers were considerable. So large a bronze vessel from that period has no like among other European finds. It must have been made on commission. This makes it clear that there existed permanent, secure links between the 'barbarian' world and the eastern Mediterranean, perhaps using Alpine passes or water courses along the Danube and the Rhône and Saône. We must also take into account the flourishing port of Massilia, present-day Marseille. The crater would have been transported in parts and will then have been put together from the sections which are still clearly marked in Greek lettering. It is quite possible that a Greek master accompanied the vessel and gave it its final form on reaching its destination.

We possess written reports that Greek workshops produced such commodities. The Greek historian Herodotus (c. 484 — after 430 B.C.) describes how the Lacedaemonians presented King Croesus of Lydia with a brass crater of equal size to that found at Vix. Similar but smaller vessels were found at Trebenište near Lake Ohrid in Yugoslavia and in the Soviet Union near the Black Sea. Another such crater is deposited in the Antiquarium in Munich. Thanks to the find at Vix we now possess a monumental example of Greek toreutics.

This magnificent example of Greek metal-work, however, must not lead us to

15   Ficoroni Cist found at Praeneste in Italy. End of 4th century B.C. Height 53 cm. Museo Nazionale di Villa Giulia, Rome.

Châtillon-sur-Seine in the Côte-d'Or mountains archeologist J. M. R. Joffroy excavated in 1953 a tomb of a 35-year old Celtic princess or priestess. Under the immense barrow, 42 metres in diameter and 6 metres in height, a tomb covering 9 square metres had been built. In the tomb lay a female body adorned with jewels, among them a gold diadem weighing 480 grammes. In the northwestern corner of the tomb stood a large bronze vessel, assume that pots and household utensils were made of such valuable material. Articles of daily use were made of baked clay and wood in Greece. Objects made of copper and bronze were chiefly those used in religious cults as gifts for temples. Only the truly wealthy households could afford bronze or copper utensils.

Apart from votive gifts, metal work prizes won by victors of various competitions were produced. The best known today is Lysicrates' monument found in Athens at the foot of the Acropolis and made as a pedestal for a bronze tripod. It was made on the orders of Lysicrates, a choregos, when his choir won a song competition of Attic tribes in the year 334 B.C. The bronze tripod was the victor's prize in the competition.

Another example is a bronze hydria which, according to the inscription it bears, was a prize during games held in honour of the goddess Hera at Argos between the year 460 and 450 B.C. The hydria and the tripod were not objects specially made only as prizes for victors. Such a tripod is a three-legged base for a cauldron. It was originally intended for heating water over the fire. The hydria was a large water jug. Tripods were made both from bronze and from pottery.

Another typical object of the Greek world was the mirror, which, for women's use, was richly decorated. The mirror is identical in appearance and made of the same material throughout Antiquity. The Greek mirror, like the Egyptian one, was made of polished bronze in the shape of a disk, with its centre often silver-plated. This disk was affixed to a handle or base. The handle or base was often in the shape of a figure, mostly that of Aphrodite.

Smaller mirrors had lids to protect the reflective surface. The reverse side of the disk or lid was adorned either with relief or engraved scenes from Greek mythology or Greek legends, and for that reason they are not only of artistic significance but reveal a good deal of history and culture. They offer an insight to Greek life, illustrating for instance the ways of dressing and the appearance of furniture, household utensils and weapons.

Bronze was used for other articles of the Greek household. The Greek house did not have a great deal of furniture. The Greeks made do with tables, seats, beds, reclining chairs and instead of cupboards they used chests. No wooden Greek furniture has survived. With the aid of pictures on vases, wall paintings, etc. we are able to reconstruct the individual types of furniture using the surviving metal parts. Luxury furniture was fixed together with bronze attachments, and it was also inlaid with ivory, silver or bronze. Entire pieces of furniture made of bronze have survived, including tables of all kinds, which were light and could easily be moved. Beds had metal frames with leather strips or ropes on which skin covers or carpets were laid, and three-legged seats were made of bronze, many with lovely ornaments. Not enough furniture has survived to enable us to reconstruct their development and thus trace changes in taste and purpose of furniture in ancient Greece.

Before leaving the world of ancient Greece mention should be made of medical instruments, which were often made of bronze and also of iron, steel or bone. The oldest surviving medical instruments date from the fifth century B.C. They are surprisingly purposefully designed, and it is

Ornamental motifs on bronze objects from the La Tène period.

16 Bronze scales found at Pompeii. Photo Fabrizio Parisio, Naples.

quite clear that in their production, attention was paid to being able to keep them clean.

Now let us turn our attention to the Apennine Peninsula where, since the eighth century B.C., the Etruscans had settled. They gave their name to Etruria, or its Latin version Tuscana, present-day Tuscany.

The history of the Etruscans has been divided into individual stages, and in the arts we can divide the developments chronologically. In the oldest period Etruscan art developed under the influence of Oriental patterns. This is the period roughly from 700 to 625 B.C. From 625 one can speak of a strong Greek influence. In the years 575 to 475 B.C. Etruscan art reached its climax, then a gradual decline set in and from the third century

B.C. it merged with Roman art. Generally it can be said that the Etruscans did not share the Greek idea of harmony and beauty. They put more vitality and harshness into their art.

Etruscan craft production reached a high level. It includes the work of bronze-makers, who produced a remarkable variety of products. The bronze industry was based on local resources. In the vicinity of the towns of Volaterae, Vetulania, Ruselae and the harbour town of Populonia (Etruscan Popluna) copper was mined and near Populonia there were also tin deposits. The Etruscans used bronze to make vessels and various objects by forging, hammering and engraving. Apart from tripods and candlesticks they became famous for the production of mirrors and cists or caskets. The shape of

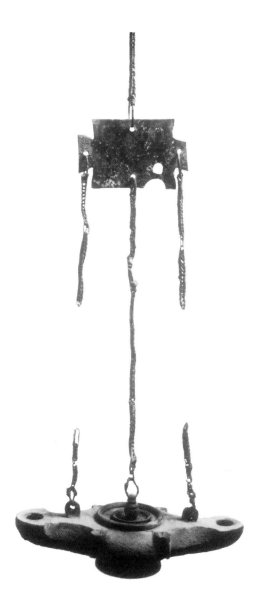

the mirrors corresponded to Greek mirrors, and most of the ornaments were engraved, though sometimes they appear in relief. More than two thousand mirrors have survived from the fifth to third centuries B.C. alone, because they were placed in women's graves. The influence of Greece is clearly visible in the production of these mirrors. The ornamental subjects are generally taken from Greek mythology.

Another object that deserves attention is the casket. This term refers to a toilet chest. They were hammered of thin bronze plate and were made in the eastern parts of the Po lowlands in the Late Bronze Age. They were called 'ciste a cordoni' (ribbed cist) since their outer surface was adorned with horizontally hammered ribs, between which there would be hammered or engraved ornaments. This type was widespread in Istria and was frequently exported across the Alps into the Carpathian lowlands. A variant of the original cists were products that came from Etruscan Bologna and from the territory of present-day Venice. In Etruria proper there probably was no such production, but these receptacles were popular throughout Europe. Finds show that they were exported as far as Lake Ladoga and to the shores of the Baltic Sea.

Cone-shaped pails were known as *situla*. Bronze situlas with strip ornaments were produced in northern Etruria in the sixth and fifth centuries B.C., and they

17 Bronze oil lamp found at Herculaneum. Photo Fabrizio Parisio, Naples.

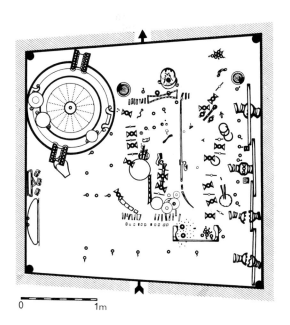

Ground plan of the tomb of a princess at Vix, France. The large Greek bronze crater in the upper left-hand corner.

0   1m

18 Bronze stand for heating device found at Pompeii. Photo Fabrizio Parisio, Naples.

spread to northern Italy and the southeastern Alpine region. Rich figural ornaments show us festive processions, sport matches or merry drinking parties of contemporary North Italian society. One famous bronze situla was found where the present-day Bologna cemetery, the Certosa di Bologna, is today. A burial place from the sixth and fifth century B.C. was found here, from the time when the Etruscan town of Felsina flourished, the predecessor of Bologna. The walls of the Certosa situla are adorned with relief scenes. In the upper part there are infantry men, in the middle strip, men and women preparing drinks and food for banquet, with musicians and guests. The lower frieze has figures of legendary gryphs.

Equally well-known are bronze situlas found at Kuffern (N. Donau) and at Watsch (Krain).

The Etruscans also made bronze furniture like the Greeks. Several three-legged tables with figures of dancers have survived. A bronze armchair, previously dated to the sixth century B.C., found at Chiusi and now in the Museum of Art in Philadelphia, was shown to be a modern forgery when it was restored in 1978.

The Romans were direct heirs to Etruscan culture. Continuous settlements of Italy from prehistory can be traced through excavations. The Alps were never an obstacle for other individual ethnic groups which intermingled with settled tribes, and this makes a highly varied picture of the early historical period. The most numerous tribes on the Apennine Peninsula were the Indo-Europeans.

It has rightly been asserted that the Romans were, essentially, peasants and soldiers, interested in practical things, and with less regard for the arts. Etruscan art, whose culminating period occurred in the sixth century B.C., had a basic influence on the beginnings of Roman art. Rome followed the Greek arts from the middle of the second century B.C. Their military successes in Greece were reflected in the Romans adopting Hellenistic art, first in the form of military loot, later by employing Greek artists in Italy.

Roman art proper developed under strong Etruscan and Greek influences. Roman art was not a unified art form. On the contrary, especially in the provinces, it was under considerable pressure from local traditions. This gave rise to regional features, which were the foundations of the art of the early Middle Ages in Europe. Most Roman art was official such as those works that served the imperial court, the central institutions and the army. Its main purpose was to represent the state and to glorify the empire and its power.

Naturally, the Etruscan influence showed in the production of bronze objects. Most of the Italian cists are similar to Etruscan cists being cylindrical, occasionally oval or square, but in contrast to the Etruscan examples they have legs, usually in the form of animals. Normally there is a lid and a handle, mostly shaped as a small sculpture. Rings attached to the body of the vessel served for the attachment of strips, rope or chains with which the vessels could be more easily carried. The outer casing of these caskets was decorated with engraved or hammered friezes with ornamental or figural subjects, usually mythological.

The cists were used mostly by women for their toilet articles or bath requirements. The type of cist that has been described is called the Praenestan type after the town of Praeneste in Latium (present-day Palestrine), where, in a burial place from the fourth and third centuries B.C. cists of this type have been unearthed. The town, which from the fifth century B.C. belonged to the Romans, was famous for the production of other high quality bronze articles, too, e.g. metal mirrors. The most famous of the Praenestan cists is the Cista Ficoroni, which derived its name from an antiquities merchant, Francesco Ficoroni, who presented it to the Jesuit college in Rome in 1745. It was found at Praeneste in 1738. Today it is in the Museo Nazionale di Villa Giulia in Rome. It is 53 cm high and on the casing has an engraving framed by two strips of ornament depicting scenes from the Argonauts set in a landscape background. The central scene depicts the landing of the Argonauts among the Bebrycans and the punishment of their King Amycus. The lid of the vessel, with a handle in the shape of three figures bears the inscription: 'Novios Plautios med Romai fecid. Dindia Macolnia fileai dedit' (Novius Plautius made me in Rome. Dindia Macolnia gave it to his daughter or, to the daughter of Malconia).

To judge by the style of the figure and the free-flowing composition, which can be compared with paintings on Apulian vases from the second half of the fourth century B.C., the Ficoroni cist can be dated to the end of the fourth or the early third century B.C.

Etruscan situlas evolved into Roman pails with rich figural decorations and double handles. Outstanding examples of

Greek bronze crater from the tomb of the princess at Vix, France.

34

this type of bronze vessel include a pail with silver-plated handles found in Pompeii and bearing the name of its owner, Cornelia Chelidoni. Pails from the Roman provinces have a slightly different shape, e.g. the Danubian Celtic vessel found in Germany near the village of Eisleben.

These vessels were used for special occasions and were therefore made of a valuable material — bronze. Receptacles for current use were generally made of baked clay as famous potter's workshops in Etruria and southern Italy prove. Excavations at Pompeii have provided insight into the equipment of ancient kitchens and given us a precise idea of Roman crockery. It is clear at first sight that most of the utensils and tools such as pans, mortars, spoons, ladles and baking forms, pots, etc. served, almost unchanged, down to the Middle Ages and do so even in the modern European kitchen. The material used for ancient kitchen utensils and tableware depended on the financial situation of the owners. One can find clay pots and also pots made of copper and bronze. Tableware and receptacles in rich households were made of valuable material such as silver, gold, glass, alabaster or onyx.

Bronze was used in Roman households outside the kitchen. It was often used to make furniture. As with the Greeks the Romans did not like too much furniture in their houses. The basic pieces of furniture in a Roman home were reclining chairs (*lectus*), which served for resting and sleeping. The Romans even used them when they were eating, a custom adopted via Greece from the Orient. Most of these chairs were made of wood, and they were decorated with bronze ornaments. Sometimes they were wholly made of bronze. Similarly tables were made of various materials, including bronze. The Roman house had several types of chairs without backs (*sella*), usually with a cushion, which could be folded and moved easily. The armchair (*solium*) always had a back support. In addition there were long and narrow benches (*scamna, subsellia*). Like the Greeks, the Romans placed their garments in chests (*arca*) while cupboards (*armarium*) were used mainly by craftsmen and traders. Some of this furniture was also made of bronze. Bronze chests served as safes, as shown by finds at Pompeii. Other objects, too, were made of bronze including door-knockers or bronze keys for door-locks. In public squares this material was used for fountains, though most of these are the work of sculptors. In Pompeii bronze heaters for water and other liquids were found in the form of a cylindrical receptacle standing on a rectangular base with legs in the shape of winged sphinxes with lion paws. To heat smaller rooms the Romans used pans or little moveable stoves, on the top of which a kettle could also be placed to heat water. Bronze and pottery were popular materials for these heaters, because they could be richly decorated.

Household equipment inevitably included lighting facilities. In the whole of Antiquity these were very primitive and gave a poor or inadequate light. Leaving

Types of ancient Greek vessels

Crater

Lekythos

Amphora

aside resinous wood, which was the oldest material for lighting, the basic light source was the oil lamp, filled with olive oil. Pottery and bronze were the most suitable materials for such oil lamps. The shape of the lamp grew smaller in the course of time; Greek ones were globular, Byzantine lamps of pear shape, but there was no technical progress. Sometimes several oil lamps were joined together to provide better light as shown by finds in Pompeii. Some improvement was brought by the use of candles, which appeared in Rome in the first century B.C. and may have been an Etruscan invention. The Greeks did not know of candles. The candles were placed into holders, and this gave rise to candlesticks or large stands called candelabrum in Latin. Bronze was used to make these. Most of the candlesticks for the household had an established shape, a tall stem on three feet.

In Antiquity bronze was a common alloy. It depended only on the financial resources of the customer whether an object was made of cheaper or more expensive material. The cupola of the Pantheon in Rome, for instance, commissioned by Emperor Hadrian in the years A.D. 115—125, was covered with tiles of gilded bronze. In the year 662 Emperor Constantine IV had these tiles removed to Constantinople. The bronze-covered door of the Pantheon, too, is of ancient date, the third century A.D. The rectangular bronze panels framed by thick ledges give the impression of a grille firmly attached to the wooden construction of the door. On these panels are heads of the Medusa, lions, etc. Other surviving examples, and occasional mentions by ancient writers, include the door of a first century circular building on the Forum in Rome, church of Hagia Sophia in Constantinople from Late Antiquity also confirm that bronze doors were common on important buildings.

As time passed, centres came into existence which grew famous for the production of bronze articles. In the south of Italy one such centre was the harbour town of Tarentum (present-day Taranto) where the bronze industry flourished when it was resettled by Dorian settlers from Laconia in the eighth century B.C. The town occupied the site of a former Mycenaean trading station. Works from this bronze industry were unearthed in tombs, among them a bronze belt from Noicattaro, today in the museum at Bari. Another high point can be dated to the second half of the fifth century B.C., and it lasted into the Hellenistic period at the turn of the era. Tarentum introduced Hellenistic art to Italy, as shown by Pompeii and Rome. Certain important works of Tarentum bronze have survived, including a bronze crater found at Derveni, today in the Museum at Thessalonica, and a bronze tub with a scene of 'Dionysius and his Followers', now in the Museum of Fine Arts in Boston, U.S.A.

Another centre of bronze production was the town of Capua, now called S. Maria di Capua Vetere. Originally it was the centre of Etruscan power but,

Amphora

Kantharos

Hydria

19 Ancient oil lamp decorated with a relief of a jumping stag. Length 13 cm. Museum of Decorative Arts, Prague.

from the fifth century B.C., it was ruled by the Samnites. In the middle of the 4th century B.C. it sought the protection of Rome. Capua became famous for its bronze tubs, situlas, kettles with handles, pans with long handles, etc. Until the second century A.D. Capuan bronze products were exported in large numbers to the Balkans and also to the territory lying north of the Alps. Then their place was taken by the developing workshops in Gaul and along the lower reaches of the Rhine.

The technology used in ancient Italy included turning bronze objects on a wooden core, for which the Romans became famous. This technology was known from the fourth century B.C., and it was used for most of the bronze vessels exported to other parts of Europe.

Before we leave the world of Antiquity let us take a brief look at collectors in Rome. The Romans greatly valued

bronze. They were good at recognising its quality and they paid considerable sums for quality pieces. Most reports on bronze come from Pliny the Elder. His *Naturalis historia,* finished in A.D. 77, represents a valuable source of information.

Individual types of bronze were mostly named after the town of origin or the colour of the alloy. Thus 'aes Aegineticum' came from the town Aegina on the western shores of the island of that name. The town became famous for its production of bronze objects and for casting bronze statues. A bronze of similar colour as 'aes Aegineticum', which is liver-brown and therefore sometimes called 'hepatizon', was bronze from the island of Delos. 'Aes Deliacum' was highly valued and added to the popularity of this island in the Cyclads that was sacred to the Greeks. 'Aes nigrum' was bronze of dark colour mentioned by the Greek writer Philostratus. The most renowned of ancient

20 Bronze oil lamp in the shape of a sailing boat symbolizing the Church. Italy, 4th century. Photo Soprintendenza Archaeologica per la Toscana, Florence.

bronzes was Corinthian bronze ('aes Corinthiaticum') and Pliny distinguished three types: the first type called 'candidum' was of light colour and is said to have contained silver. Pliny was convinced that the second type, of golden colour, originated by the addition of gold to the alloy. The third type contained an additive of a small quantity of different metals. Modern analytical methods have not confirmed Pliny's claims, and it seems likely that the concept of the addition of precious metals in Corinthian bronze was only a trick by clever merchants. It can be assumed that in the case of Pliny's gold bronze we are dealing with brass. The Romans, however, were well acquainted with the technology of gilding by fire, and probably could gild bronze with gold plate.

In the fifth century A.D. the pressure of barbarians against the Roman Empire intensified and the process of disintegration was speeded up by internal crises supported by popular uprisings. 'Barbarian kingdoms' were established in territories of the Empire including the Visigoths in Hispania in A.D. 418, the Vandals in Africa in A.D. 429, while a Burgundian kingdom emerged on the Rhône in A.D. 443. This process reached its culmination with the deposition of the last Emperor of the Western Empire, Romulus Augustulus, in A.D. 476 by the leader of the barbarian mercenaries, Odoacer, who reigned in Italy as king and sent the emblems of imperial power to Constantinople. This was the end of the Western Roman Empire both formally and de facto. For the eastern part of the Empire the end of the world of Antiquity is often dated to A.D. 529, when the 'pagan' philosophical school in Athens was finally closed.

The Migration of Nations and Byzantine Art

European art can be divided into two sections. In the East the traditions of Antiquity continued unbroken under the protection of the still powerful Eastern Roman Empire. Its cultural and political centre was Constantinople. Here artists were able to work without interruption even though, as we shall see, some events had a negative effect on the arts.

In the territory of the Western Roman Empire matters were different. In the fifth century A.D. a widespread migration of Germanic and Slavic nations reached its apex in Europe north of the Alps. The migrating peoples moved from the north and east of Europe to the west and south as far as the Iberian and the Apennine peninsulas and the north of Africa. This may have been stimulated by changes in the European climate and the pressure of Mongolian tribes, the Huns. The chain reaction caused by this Mongolian influx changed the image of Europe considerably. Roman Gaul was occupied principally by the Germanic Franks during the fifth century. They founded the Frankish Empire under the Merovingian dynasty. In A.D. 486 the Germanic Ostrogoths invaded the Apennine Peninsula and founded the Ostrogoths Empire around Ravenna, which became the capital of their new empire. In the northern part of the peninsula the Langobards began to settle in A.D. 568. The Slavs, in their penetration of central Europe, reached the Elbe in the north, occupied the large territory of former Pannonia in the south and migrated as far as the coast of the Adriatic Sea. This tempestuous period has rightly been regarded as the beginning of a new epoch in the history of Europe.

For European history of art the contact between the Germanic and Asian artistic feelings proved of remarkable significance. It was due to the mingling of the Scythians and the Sarmatian traditions that these two attitudes to art gave rise to 'Germanic barbarian' art. Through migration, this new art spread throughout Europe. A characteristic feature of this art is geometrical ornament and a fondness for precious materials.

Bronze, brass and copper did not play an important role during these migrations, but they did acquire a new function. Almost all efforts of the craftsmen of the time were centred on the production of jewellery and ornamental objects, among them the popular fibulas, brooches, buckles and clasps in the shape of stylized birds — perhaps eagles or crows, the companions of the Germanic gods Hugin and Munin. These objects were richly decorated with coloured enamel made in various goldsmiths' techniques such as *cloissonné* or *champlevé* enamel. The base was mostly copper, only in the case of the most luxurious object was gold applied. Thus bronze and copper became a substitute for other precious metals. With a general shortage of gold and silver, bronze and particularly copper took their place in the production of sacred utensils.

The eastern part of the Roman Empire at first experienced less dramatic events even though the barbarians, including the Germani, Bulgars and Slavs, had to be driven away. The art of Late Antiquity continued and gradually evolved into Byzantine art. The Hellenistic and Roman beginnings were never suppressed in Byzantine art, and several intentional returns to the past supported this traditionalism. Under no circumstances can Byzantine art be viewed as lacking progress, but compared with Western art the changes were less striking and more difficult to perceive. It must also be taken into account that Byzantine art left its mark retrospectively. European pre-Romanesque

21   Bronze grille in Charlemagne chapel in
Aachen cathedral. Germany, early 9th
century. Photo Ann Münchow, Aachen.

22   Bronze aquamanile from Hradec
Králové, Bohemia. Lower Saxony, second
half of 13th century. Height 26.5 cm.
National Museum, Prague.

23   Detail of the handle of the aquamanile
from Hradec Králové.

24 Gothic brass
candlestick. Kutná Hora,
Bohemia. Height 17.5 cm.
Museum of Decorative Arts,
Prague.

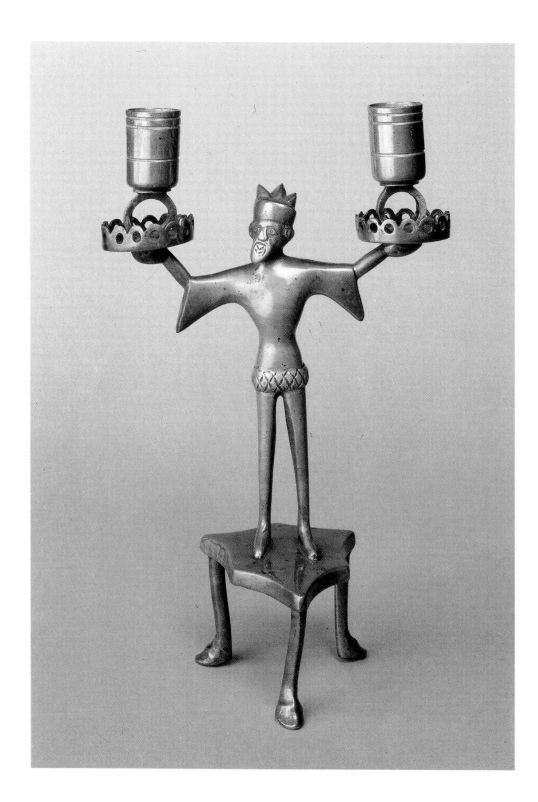

25   Bronze table candlestick with a figural stem. Central Europe, 15th century. Height 24 cm. National Museum, Prague.

26   Bronze baptismal font with copper lid. Slovakia, 1497. Height 100 cm. Parish church at Spišské Vlachy, Slovakia.

44

45

28   Two Gothic candlesticks from the
church at Plzenec and at Lovčice in
Bohemia. 15th century. Height 25 and
28 cm. National Museum, Prague.

27   Bronze baptismal font
with later copper lid.
Slovakia, 1549. Height
105 cm. Parish church at
Spišská Nová Ves, Slovakia.

29 Bronze mortar. The upper edge bears the inscription 'ave+maria+gracia+plena+ominus'. The outer side of the mortar has the letter 'W' below a crown and the year 1490. Bohemia. Height 23 cm. Museum of Decorative Arts, Prague.

and Romanesque art often found inspiration and strength from the art that came from Constantinople.

Constantinople grew from a small unimportant village of Greek colonists on the shores of the Bosporus, called Byzantion in Greek. Constantine I intended to build an Empire of New Rome in the East as shown by the name of the town in one imperial decree. The rich Roman families either moved voluntarily into the town or were forced to do so. Immense building activity followed, giving rise to grand palaces for rich patricians and public colonial buildings. The only structure that survives is the Hagia Sophia, the church of Holy Wisdom. Byzantine culture as a whole underwent several periods of success followed by times of stagnation. Throughout the existence of the Byzantine Empire Constantinople was a town of magnificence and luxury, as shown by the historian Procopius, who lived during Emperor Justinian's reign. The same is true of Constantine VII Porphyrogenitus, one of the emperors of the tenth century, who wrote a book on ceremonies, which contains descriptions of the magnificent palaces of Constantinople. The arts and crafts were of a high standard as the few surviving objects indicate. Otherwise we know little about them. When the Turks conquered the town in 1453 the churches and palaces were reconstructed or destroyed, and nothing has survived of the interior furnishings. Nor do we know much more of the average dwellings of the citizens of Constantinople, or of the interior of a Byzantine household. Thus we cannot now know what role bronze played in the daily life of Constantinople.

It is, however, clear that bronze casting continued to flourish in Byzantium and became famous throughout the Mediterranean region. The best examples are bronze doors. Under the influence of Byzantium or perhaps as direct import from Constantinople a group of bronze doors were installed in southern Italy. The oldest example is the door of the cathedral at Amalfi (1060 — 66). Others are to be found at Salerno, Trani, Monte S. Angelo and elsewhere. Typical of this group are ornamented metal plates into which silver or other metal fibres have been hammered (a technique known as niello). The inlay forms ornamental or figural decorations, mostly with subjects from the life of Christ or legends of the saints. Similarly the Byzantine influence spread far to the northeast, to Russia, where we find a related group of bronze doors. The oldest is that at Suzdal (1230 — 33). The Russian doors have richer ornamentation in niello and stress is placed on relief framing of the individual sections or panels. A strong Byzantine influence can be seen on a later bronze door in Italy. Here niello was replaced by basrelief, but the division of the door and the manner of framing is still based on Byzantine patterns. Typical of this group is the work of Bonannus of Pisa (cathedral at Pisa, 1140 — 50, cathedral at Monreale, 1186) and Barisanus of Trani (Trani, c. 1190, Ravello, 1179). This group includes the door of the cathedral at Augsburg in Germany (1050 — 60), which may have been made in a Byzantine workshop. The door of the cathedral at Hildesheim belongs to a different group, which will be discussed later.

Among small objects there are interesting bronze crosses with figural motifs engraved or in relief, mostly of Christ with arms outstretched on the obverse and the Virgin Mary or another saint on the reverse. The saints are shown in a posture of prayer with open arms raised. The small crosses are usually two-sided, with a hollow or opening to hold a relic. They were cast and had a ring at the upper end from which they could be hung. These were souvenirs that pilgrims could purchase on their journey to the Holy Land. The oldest pieces dating from the sixth and seventh centuries came from Syria and Palestine. In later centuries there was an increase in pilgrimages and these little crosses became so popular that they began to be produced in other parts of Europe, and local influences began to show in their shape and ornamentation. Basically, it can be said that all these little crosses follow Byzantine patterns. This is clear from their figural and decorative ornaments and is particularly true of the figure of Christ. Until the ninth century it was customary in the entire Christian world to depict Christ alive, standing, wearing a loin cloth, with outstretched arms in front of the cross on a step designed as a footrest. In Byzantium it is more usual to depict Christ dressed in a sleeveless tunic, the colobium. The Western European crosses are usually cast in one piece, they have no aperture to hold a relic and have decoration only on one side. It is very difficult to date individual pieces since the type and ornamentation of the crosses did not change over the centuries for traditional reasons until the end of the eleventh century when their popularity rapidly declined. These little crosses were scattered all over Europe since the stream of pilgrims went to Palestine along several routes.

Special types of bronze crosses were the Kievan crosses, which came into use shortly before the conquest of Kiev by the Mongols in 1240. Stone moulds of crosses have been found in the area of the town, and one casting was found in a tunnel in St Michael's monastery built by the citizens of the town in an attempt to escape from the siege. One of these crosses was discussed by Z. Lovag. It was found on the territory of what is today Hungary, where it will have been taken by the citizens of Kiev seeking refuge from the Tartars. On the front there is the figure of Christ, at the end of the bar of the cross, in circular medallions, are relief busts of the Virgin Mary, John the Evangelist, St Nicholas and St George. On the reverse side is the Virgin Mary and busts of St Peter, St Basle, St Cosmas and St Damian. The inscription in Cyrillic lettering shows its Kievan origin. On the front below the arms of Christ there is an inscription which in translation reads: 'The Cross is our magnificence, the Cross is our consolation.' On the other side: 'Holy Mother of God, stand by us.'

The Middle Ages

The Middle Ages is a customary, though not precise term, for the period in European history from the fifth to the end of the fifteenth century A.D. In the history of art it is further subdivided on the basis of the styles that predominated at various times. These terms came into existence mainly at a much later period and were coined in the main by scholars.

We have already seen that the 'barbarian' peoples who occupied parts of the disintegrating Western Roman Empire brought with them a culture where the stress of artistic work was on decorative crafts. This form of art absorbed stimuli from Greek and Roman provincial art and drew heavily on the treasure houses of the Oriental steppe peoples. The Germanic flat and abstract form was popular among the Langobards, Goths and Franks. As it moved across Europe, it encountered the art of the Celts and Romans. The adoption of Christianity did little to suppress this ornamental art, which reached a high degree of technical perfection, as shown by the works of Gothic and Frankish goldsmiths. It spread over large parts of Europe, in the south as far as the Iberian Peninsula, westwards to Ireland and north to Scandinavia, where the Vikings prolonged its existence to the end of the first millennium.

This influx of barbarian art virtually overpowered Roman art. The lesson of Rome was respected only in architecture, epitomised by the building of new churches linked with the spread of Christianity. The craftsmen of that period, especially in the Merovingian Empire, reached a high level of workmanship in making objects of precious metals. Products of bronze or copper, however, are virtually unknown to us as most of them did not survive. Only in the north of Europe have unique Viking products survived. Even this art was suppressed by Charlemagne, whose cultural interests lay with the traditions of Rome.

Charlemagne was mostly concerned with renewing the Roman Empire in the western regions. He used art to serve his aims. Art was conceived as underscoring the might of the emperor. The artists at the court of Charlemagne willingly adopted styles from Italy and from the Byzantine East. It is significant for our theme that in the chapel of Charlemagne's imperial palace at Aachen, built at the end of the eighth century and consecrated to the

30 Bronze aquamanile found not far from a ruined medieval church in the village of Veľká Čalomija. Slovakia, early 13th century. Height 22.5 cm. Central Slovakian Museum, Banská Bystrica.

51

31 Two brass aquamaniles in the shape of lions. Lower Saxony, second half of 13th century. Height of the larger artifact 20 cm. Museum of Decorative Arts, Prague.

Virgin Mary, bronze re-appeared as an architectural feature. Witness the bronze ballustrade of the gallery above the central area and the door-knocker in the shape of a lion's head on the 'Wolf Portal'. It is known that Charlemagne summoned the most skilful workers and craftsmen from the whole Empire to work for him.

The pre-Romanesque period lasted from the fifth to the eleventh century. In the eleventh century the classical Middle Ages began in Europe, and the art that now came into being was later called Romanesque. It was based on the art of Antiquity but as it developed the artists sought their own manner of expressing the changed spiritual and social climate. The Church was the main bearer of this culture and art. The monasteries were centres from which new ideas radiated and where art was actually created. Monastery workshops dealt with a broad range

of activities, including metal work. Interest in work with bronze was once again widespread in Europe, north of the Alps, chiefly in Germany. One of the important centres was Hildesheim, several kilometres south of Hanover, where a metal-casting workshop came into existence under Bishop Bernward (993—1022). It made the town an important cultural centre in eleventh-century Germany. This workshop stimulated new interest in bronze-casting in the eleventh and twelfth centuries in the whole of Central Europe, which led some scholars to coin the term the 'Second Bronze Age'.

Though we can hardly imagine Bernward's workshop without the influence, at least in technical matters, of Italy and through its mediation, of Byzantium, the technical achievements of this workshop truly deserve our admiration. One of the monumental works made there is a double bronze door for the church of St

32 The Gloucester candlestick. Cast in rare copper, silver, zinc, lead and tin alloys in three parts (foot, stem and drip-tray), which are linked by an iron rod. One of the inscriptions reveals the origin of the candlestick: 'Abbatis Petri gregis et devotio mitis me dedit ecclesie sci Petri Gloecestere'. England, 12th century. Height 58.4 cm. Victoria and Albert Museum, London.

Bronze pail with a movable
handle, *c.* 1500.

33   Bronze sanctuary ring on the door of
the St Wenceslas Chapel in St Vitus'
Cathedral in Prague. Alleged to have been
originally on the door of the church in Stará
Boleslav where Wenceslas was assassinated.
Bohemia (?), second half of 12th century.
Diameter of circular plate 51 cm. Photo
A. Paul, Prague.

Michael (today Hildelsheim cathedral). Work on this door was probably begun in 1015. Each section weighs almost four tons and is 4.72 by 1.20 m wide. It is cast in one piece. Both folds are decorated with eight relief panels illustrating biblical scenes. On the left fold there are scenes from the Old Testament, of the creation of Eve to Cain and Abel. The right-hand fold shows scenes from the New Testament, the life and death of Christ. The Hildesheim reliefs hold an important place in the development of medieval European art. The reliefs range from a flat treatment of the architectonic background to low relief and finally to three dimensional portrayal, e.g. the heads of the figures. In its artistic treatment the door forms only the base for the reliefs with less emphasis on the individual panels ground. Some details of the reliefs are chased. It is assumed that the reliefs were inspired by Carolingian book painting and ivory carvings. A narrow band on each fold of the door bears the inscription,

clearly of later date, that the door was made by Bishop Bernward in 1015 to the great glory of the Lord and as his own memorial. One record suggests that the door was finished and placed on site only after the good Bishop's death in 1022.

Another major work by Bishop Bernward in the same cathedral (and also originally intended for St Michael's) is an almost four metre high bronze column made between 1015 and 1022. Following the pattern of the ancient Column of Trajan in Rome it has relief decorations along a spiral strip with 28 scenes from the life of Christ. Originally the top had a capital but that was destroyed in the seventeenth century. It was to have held the 'cereus paschalis', a big candle, which is blessed in a catholic church for the Easter vigil and which then stands by the altar until Ascension Day. This ancient custom, dating to the fourth century A.D., was the symbol of the resurrection of Christ as the Light of the World.

The art of the Hildesheim school spread to Saxony in the early eleventh century, and in the twelfth century the centre of bronze production shifted to Magdeburg. The Magdeburg master Riquinus made the bronze door at Novgorod (1152—4) in Russia. In artistic concept it is based on an older pattern and did not follow the more progressive workmanship of the Hildesheim craftsmen. The reliefs are once again placed in panels with ornamental frames.

In the eleventh and twelfth centuries there was a growing network of monasteries with workshops where skilled craftsmen-monks were active. The degree of technological knowledge is remarkable. This was proved in a work by Theophilus *De diversis artibus* from the early twelfth century. Theophilus described himself a priest and monk. His writing with such a broad scope is quite unusual in medieval literature. The author divided his book into three parts, dealing with the most important and technologically exacting spheres of painting, the production and treatment of glass and that of metal. Painting is covered in 38 chapters, glass in 31 chapters, and he devotes as much as 96 chapters to metals. In addition, Theophilus deals with each subject systematically with the evident aim of explaining clearly the process and media as clearly as possible. The author, clearly, acquaints the

34 Hansa dish with relief bust of the Ottonian Emperor on the crossing of the two ornamental strips with relief vines. Magdeburg (?), 12th century. Diameter 30 cm. Staatliche Galerie Moritzburg, Halle.

reader with the things with which he was in constant and practical contact. The description of the materials and their qualities, the equipment of the workshop and the tools imply great expert knowledge. The writer must have had practical experience in dealing with metals. Theophilus's work gives us an insight into the early medieval monastery workshops and shows their high level, especially in technology. The period when only the monasteries had at their disposal craftsmen-specialists, however, was coming to an end.

A new factor emerged in European history in the Gothic period. The medieval towns were emerging and with them a new type of inhabitant, the burgher. Obviously the monastery workshops could not satisfy the needs of the growing towns, nor were they interested in doing so as they produced mostly objects for their own use, such as baptismal fonts, censers, altar crosses, candlesticks, etc. The monastery workshops ceased to be the only centres of craftsmanship. The town workshops slowly took over the initiative. As very little material has survived, we can hardly speak of bronze or copper objects for domestic use in the twelfth century. In most homes utensils made of wood or clay were probably used. But brass began to be worked on a larger scale in twelfth century Europe. The town of Dinant in the Maas valley in present-day Belgium held an almost monopoly status in the production of brass objects by the end of the twelfth century. It was encouraged by rich deposits of zinc ore in the Maas valley and

could look back on an ancient tradition of brass production in the region. Products from Dinant were sold all over Europe so that the term Dinanderie came into general use in certain countries, among them France, to describe objects made of brass.

The area of Dinant lies on territory bordered by the diocese of Liège, i.e. from the mouth of the R. Maas to the southern Ardennes and from the town of Löwen to Aachen. Several factors contributed to the development of art in that area. In the first place, the raw material deposits of iron and calamine, building limestone and supplies of timber. The river and relatively good roads dating back to the time of Rome, provided transport routes that linked ports with deposits of copper in the Harz mountains and in Lower Saxony. The transport of tin from the British Isles was easy, too.

The rich harbour towns supported art so that one can speak of Maas art, which flourished from the end of the eleventh century to the middle of the thirteenth century. This term includes the art of metal-casting as well as book painting, sculpture and ivory carving. Maas art drew on stimuli provided by trade links from the Rhineland, France, Italy and Byzantium as well as the Arab world.

Bronze work is a good example of Maas art. One fine work is the bronze baptismal font in the church of Saint-Barthélemy in Liège made between the years 1107 and 1118. Traditionally it is attributed to Master Reiner, a burgher of Huy, who, on a list issued by the Bishop of

Gothic jug from the 15th century.

Gothic jug on three legs, turn of 14th to 15th century.

35   Bronze censer with figural Bible scenes of the three Youths in the Fiery Oven on the lid. France, 12th century. Palais des Beaux-Arts, Lille.

Liège in 1125, is given as 'Reinerus auri-faber'. The font is in the shape of a cylin-drical vessel with walls adorned with five relief scenes related to baptism including the baptism of Christ. Ten of the original 12 figures of beasts holding the dish of consecrated water have survived. This composition may have been inspired by a metal dish described in the Old Testa-ment that used to stand in the forecourt of the temple of Solomon. It was used by the priests for washing before the service and was called 'a metal sea'. Here, too, the metal dish was upheld by twelve beasts symbolizing the twelve tribes of Israel (Old Testament, Book of Kings I, 7, 23—26). The Liège font also has inscriptions linking the beasts to the 12 Apostles. From the point of view of form, it is clear that Master Reiner was influenced in or-namenting the font by the art of Antiqui-ty, via Byzantium. This influence is particularly clear on the scene of the baptism of Christ. Reiner's work left a profound mark on contemporary art and found many followers. To name but a few, the altar cross, today in the Victoria and Albert Museum, or the well-known bronze baptismal font in the Palais des Beaux-Arts in Lille.

The bronze baptismal font is a monumental work. In the early Middle Ages it was customary to baptize by immersion, and the font had to be adequately sized.

36 Bronze candlestick in the shape of a man riding a lion. Maas river basin, 12th century. 32×25 cm. Musée des Arts Décoratifs, Paris.

When, in the thirteenth century, baptism by infusion was generally introduced, baptismal fonts were made with smaller water dishes on higher legs or pedestals. The basic forms of fonts became settled in the early Middle Ages. They were in the shape of a cylindrical or polygonal tub or a basin-shaped dish resting on a column with a figuraly shaped or stem-shaped foot. The font with a dish in the manner of a chalice resting on a knopped stem was highly popular in the Carpathians, from the mining towns of today's Slovakia to the Romanian towns in Transylvania where this form of baptismal font was taken by German craftsmen. On the other hand, in England the current form was a polygonal baptizing vessel and in France and Belgium it was square.

Brass products from the Maas valley were not all monumental in character. There was a broad range of cast or hammered objects. Apart from candlesticks with richly adorned feet or reading lecterns in the form of eagles with spread wings most common were kettles, pans, dishes or receptacles for holy water. Dishes with engraved ornaments were exported far afield. Since most of these were transported by the Hanseatic fleet, whose widespread trading network encouraged this long-distant trade with Dinanderie, the term 'Hansaschüssel' was used in German-speaking regions. The production of articles of brass in Dinant remained important throughout the Middle Ages and lost its dominant position only in 1466 when the town was destroyed by war. It is thought that those braziers from Dinant who survived the war and left the devastated town founded a new tradition in certain other European towns, e.g. in Dutch Middelburg, in Aachen and Stolberg and mainly Nuremberg in Germany and in a number of towns in France and England.

W. Dexel realized that in this phase of the Middle Ages, i.e. from the twelfth century, bronze objects were based on the shape of wooden utensils which existed in every household. For instance, bronze tubs whose general shape was derived from wooden tubs. They even had bands around them which, on the bronze tub, became relief cast decoration. Bronze mortars initially repeated the shape of wooden mortars turned on a lathe, but later, at the time of Gothic art, they fol-

37 Half-figure of St Peter
on the bronze baptismal font
shown in colour on photo
No. 26.

Bronze was the most suitable material for such a kettle. Fourteenth century samples show a mature well-tested shape. Kettles for the fire underwent a slow development in different parts of Europe, from the globular form of the fourteenth century to wide, low or pear-shaped ones of the fifteenth and sixteenth centuries. In the seventeenth and eighteenth centuries the round shape again became widespread. With the introduction of cooking ranges these three-legged vessels gradually faded out.

Typical pieces of household equipment in richer households were brass vessels, for which the term 'Schenkkanne' was adopted in Germany. They are usually referred to as ewers in England. German specialist literature has devoted a good deal of attention to such vessels, most recently H. P. Lockner and M. Wiswe. The reason may well be that a relatively large number of them have survived. Basically they date from the fifteenth century and can be divided into two main types: typical of the first is the bell-shaped body of the vessel standing on three legs. There is an evident relationship of this type to the three-legged bronze kettles. The second type has a circular stand with a stem, on which the body proper is set. The shape is either conical, slightly widening towards the top or spherical with a fairly long neck. Those without feet usually have a lid attached to the main body with a hinge.

Technically it can be said that they show good craftsmanship. They are mostly cast by the cire perdue process and finished on the lathe. The handle and spout were cast separately and were attached to the body by soldering or brazing.

There are naturally many variations in the actual body form as in ornamentation. It is remarkable that we can trace the second type far into the nineteenth century, though, understandably, in the later periods they were made mainly from brass or copper plate, if not from pewter.

In England, too, several interesting bronze or brass vessels have survived from the Middle Ages. One of them is a ewer which held water for rinsing the hands at table. It is decorated with a relief coat-of-arms of King Richard II of England (1367—1400) and has inscriptions in Gothic lettering citing proverbs. This ewer has a loose lid without hinges. It

lowed the general vertical trends and the vertical ribs on the outside of the mortar often ended at the bottom in a lion's paw. With mortars one can distinguish a variety of shapes according to the place of origin. While in the north of Europe the mortars were cast with typical buttresses and had a strictly conical body, in Central, Western and Southern Europe mortars became popular with slightly concave walls without buttresses.

Objects of daily use included bronze kettles on three legs with a strong moveable handle for suspension. They were meant for use in an open fireplace. The kettle stood either by the fire or could be hung at the required distance above it.

38 The year 1497 on the baptismal font on colour photo No. 26. Notice the graphic form of Late Gothic numbers.

was found in 1896 in the town of Kumasi, in present-day Ghana, in the Ashanti Region and is now in the British Museum. A similar ewer with the coat-of-arms of England and an inscription, but without a lid, is the property of the Victoria and Albert Museum. These surviving pieces confirm the report that a Worshipful Company of Founders already existed in London in 1365, and its masters produced a variety of objects by casting, among them stirrups, clasps, candlesticks, jugs and pans.

A special type of water pot was developed in the Middle Ages, called an aquamanile. Such pots were used for liturgical purposes when water was poured over the hands of the priest and also in secular dining rooms. They were made to resemble a surprising wealth of subjects, e.g. figures of lions, griffins, stags, dogs, also riders on horseback, centaurs, Samson fighting the lion and the number of surviving aquamaniles (several hundred

Bronze hand warmer, which was filled with charcoal. 12th century.

pieces) show that they must have been very popular. The oldest can be dated into the twelfth century, but the majority of surviving aquamaniles come from a later period. Towards the end of the Middle Ages their popularity rapidly declined and they were replaced by kettles. Research has shown that the motif of animal figures, and with it the direct stimulus to the production of such pots must be sought in the western Islamic cultural sphere. The twelfth century was the period of the first and the second crusade, and Europe came thus into direct contact with the cultures of the East. Some scholars think that the group of aquamaniles in the shape of a rider on horseback, as found in Central Europe, cannot be included in the western European types, and they see a direct link between the Central European cultural sphere, especially Hungary, and the East without the mediating role of the West (Z. Lovag). From a formal viewpoint, the develop-

ment of the aquamaniles was rather slow over time and it can be said that the imaginative character of the subject-matter receded and they became plain and utilitarian in form.

The aquamanile was used by priests during divine service for rinsing hands. Originally, this hand-washing was attributed to the possibility that the priest might have dirtied his hands when accepting and incensing sacrificial gifts at the altar. The water used for washing was caught in a dish known as a lavabo. It is interesting in this connection that dishes of brass plate were used for this purpose in the whole of Europe. They came into existence by the middle of the thirteenth century at the latest. At that time the main centre of production lay in the Maas valley. Later this craft spread to the German lands, particularly after the destruction of Dinant in 1466. We know of numerous makers of lavabos or basins among craftsmen in Brunswick, Lübeck, Magdeburg

39   Bronze baptismal font standing on ten (originally twelve) figures of cattle and with five reliefs on the outside. Reiner van Huy, 1107—18. Church of St Bartholomew, Liège. Bildarchiv Photo Marburg.

61

41 Base of the Milan candlestick in St Vitus' Cathedral in Prague. Maas region, *c.* mid 12th century. Height 30 cm.

◁

40 Bronze baptismal font. Richly decorated on the outside and the lid with reliefs of biblical scenes and the coat-of-arms of the Hildesheim bishopric and the figure of the donor Wilbernus. Hildesheim cathedral, *c.* 1220. Height with lid 180 cm, largest diameter 103 cm. Bildarchiv Photo Marburg.

and mainly in Nuremberg. Production flourished at the end of the fifteenth century and in the early sixteenth century. After 1600 its popularity declined, except in southern Germany, and the craft of dish-maker merged with that of the coppersmith. In Nuremberg alone in 1773 and 1776 brass-founder apprentices presented such dishes as their masterpiece under the contemporary name of 'Presentir-Schale'.

As for form, these dishes or bowls can be traced from the early fifteenth century when they were quite deep with a narrow edge; they developed to a broader rim and shallower depth. Ornaments were hammered in relief. In older pieces there are simple figural motifs on the bottom, figures of stags, of women and of flowers. Later pieces have various symbolical scenes. As time passed, a noticeable decline in artistic quality set in.

The animal motif was often used in the

Middle Ages for sanctuary rings. The oldest have the shape of a lion's head holding a ring in its teeth. Such sanctuary rings show clearly that in the early Middle Ages goldsmiths were engaged in casting such objects in bronze as bronze at that time was very precious material.

Sanctuary rings were already known in Antiquity. A ring in the shape of a hand holding a stone comes from Persia. More have survived from the Middle Ages. A sanctuary ring in the form of a human face with a ring of rays around the head from about 1133 is in Durham cathedral.

Bronze was also widely used to make censers. These are some of the oldest liturgical objects as Coptic and Syrian censers have been found. Such a censer consists of the actual incense holder, mostly semi-circular in shape, suspended usually on three chains, with a perforated lid for air to keep the incense smouldering and allow the scented smoke to spread. Such

43   a) Gothic candlestick on three feet in
the shape of lion's paws. Central Europe,
15th century. Height 52 cm.
    b) Bronze candlestick with a profiled or
knopped stem. Below the little drip tray
there is a hook for the wick-cutter. Central
Europe, early 16th century. Height 45.5 cm.
Both candlesticks are in the collections of the
Museum of the City of Prague.

◁
42   Detail of the Milan
candlestick.

65

44 Bronze door knocker in the shape of a lyre composed of leaves and lizards, with the bust of the Muse in the centre. Panel in the shape of a mascaroon. Italy, 16th century. Height 34 cm. Museum of Decorative Arts, Prague.

66

45   Detail of the door knocker on colour photo No. 44.

46 Bronze mortar. The outer side has relief figures of little angels to a design by P. Flötner.
Probably work of the Prague bell-maker Brixi of Cynperk. Prague, 16th century. Height
11.5 cm. Museum of the City of Prague.

47   Detail of the ornaments on the mortar
on colour photo No. 46.

48   Bronze mortar with handles in the
shape of horses heads. On the outside, relief
ornaments of figures. Italy, 16th century.
Height 10 cm. Museum of Decorative Arts,
Prague.

49 Dish of hammered brass with a portrait
of an Emperor of Antiquity in a circular
medallion. Nuremberg, early 16th century.
Diameter 32 cm. National Museum, Prague.

50   Detail of the ornamentation of the dish
on colour photo No. 49.

51 Foot of a Romanesque candlestick found in Zábĕhlice, Prague. Bohemia, second half of 12th century. Height 8 cm. National Museum, Prague.

a censer is borne before a bishop in a procession and is used to cleanse persons and objects, in particular the altar, during divine service. Supplies of incense are brought to the altar in a special boat-shaped dish on a small foot, called a navicula.

The oldest surviving censer is from the eleventh century. At that time producers in the Maas valley were famous for making such articles. In regard to form, one can basically divide these early censers into two types, one architecturally based, the other of rounded form. A leading example of the first type is a censer in Trier cathedral in Germany. It comes from the early twelfth century. In shape it represents a round-domed building with rich figural decorations. There are figures of the prophets Aaron, Moses, Isaiah and Jeremiah and, above them, Abel, Melchizedek, Abraham sacrificing, and Jacob blessing. There is also Solomon's throne and finally Christ on the chain holder. A censer in Lille from about 1160 has a remarkable iconographic style. It is the rounded type with perforation in the form of tendrils and various animals. On the top of the lid there is an angel with the youths in the fiery oven. This censer, associated with the name of Master Reiner, is one of the most beautiful censers in existence.

Another sphere where bronze found application was lighting equipment. The preceding chapter showed that oil lamps and candles were used in Antiquity. The Middle Ages did not add much to lighting

techniques, and the torch, the oil lamp and the candle remained the chief sources of light.

Candles were widely used in the Middle Ages. In catholic liturgy the candle played a significant role as the symbol of Christ, the Light of the World. No wonder that in the early Middle Ages candlesticks had the shapes of fantastic animals, symbols of darkness and evil, which were conquered by light. The prototype of these Romanesque candlesticks are two candlesticks belonging to Abbot Bernward of Hildesheim, dating from before 1022. This type of candlestick was imitated throughout Europe, and the favourite material was bronze. That value was attributed to products of bronze in the Middle Ages as shown by a torso of a Romanesque candlestick in St Vitus' Cathedral in Prague, which is said to have been brought home by Czech warriors as loot when they helped the Emperor to conquer Milan in 1081. The foot of the candlestick is related in type and style to decorative candlesticks from the known metal foundry in the Maas valley. It is dated to before the middle of the twelfth century.

Another example of an early medieval candlestick and example of the skill of foundry-masters of the time — this time in England — is the Gloucester candlestick. Latin inscriptions tell of its origin and history. One such inscription relates that the candlestick was presented to St Peter's church in Gloucester by Abbot Peter. He was elected abbot of Gloucester Abbey in 1104. The second inscription reveals that Thomas Poche presented it as gift to the treasure of the church at Le Mans in France. When the candlestick came to France is not known, but it is thought that this may have been in the thirteenth century. In 1861 it was bought by the Victoria and Albert Museum as an example of Anglo-Norman art.

Before the end of the Middle Ages, candlesticks were made in Europe where the stem was modelled in the shape of a wild man, based on the symbolism of the Middle Ages, which conceived the world dualistically as the struggle of evil forces against the forces of good. In Christian churches, seven-armed candlesticks were used, which represent the seven gifts of the Holy Spirit in Christian symbolism. This idea that the seven-armed candelabrum depicts the tree of life and the

52 Bronze water jug with a loose lid. The body is decorated with relief ornaments consisting of the coat-of-arms of England and that of King Richard II (1367—1400), and the text of two proverbs. England, second half of 14th century. Height 61 cm. British Museum, London.

flames of the candles the stars of heaven, brought candlesticks of this type into the churches. This interpretation of the seven-armed candelabrum was adopted by the Church in the fifth century. The oldest surviving example is the Essen candlestick, made on order of Abbess Mathilde (971 — 1011), apparently in foundries of Lower Saxony. Such monumental works were similarly produced in the traditional region of brass production in the Maas valley. The best example for this is the Trivulzio candelabrum in Milan cathedral, which is dated *c.* 1200, and, in style, is related to the workshop of Nicholas of Verdun. In Greek Orthodox churches the seven-armed candelabrum is the symbol of New Israel or the Church, and it is normally placed beside the altar.

In the late Middle Ages a type of candlestick appeared that then became prevalent everywhere and was popular until

53   Bronze oil lamp in the shape of a boat. There are five holes around the centre of the lamp and it has an engraved vine ornament. Central Europe, 15th century. Museum of Decorative Arts, Prague.

the end of the sixteenth century. This candlestick stood on a circular base, out of which grew a round profiled stem ending in a fairly wide drip pan with a spike for the candle. Candlesticks of this type have survived in fairly large numbers since they were used not only in church, but also to light secular dwellings.

Another type of lighting were chandeliers suspended from the ceiling of the room. Apart from other materials here, too, brass and bronze was used. At the beginning they were simple undecorated bars in the form of a cross with candles placed at the ends. At the point where the bars crossed, a pole was affixed from which the chandelier hung from the ceiling. In the Romanesque period, a type of chandelier came into existence for which the term 'ring chandelier' was used. Such a chandelier was actually a type of crown chandelier, one with more bars and thereby greater light intensity. The ring chandelier was usually castellated with little spires and gates to symbolize the Heavenly Jerusalem. Few examples of Romanesque chandeliers have survived. The few that do exist are in Germany, where again the Hildesheim workshop played an inspiring role. A chandelier from the first third of the eleventh century, made on order of Bishop Bernward,

54 Bronze baptismal font. The Latin inscription names H. Tegetmeiger and A. Eddelendes and gives the year 1492. Height 74 cm. Parish church of St Mary, Heiligenstadt.

55 Bronze baptismal font.
Germany, 15th century.
Height 82 cm. Former
monastery church of St
Martin, Heiligenstadt.

was destroyed in the seventeenth century but using it as a pattern Master Wibertus made such a ring chandelier in 1166 for the cathedral at Aachen. The same pattern served for a ring chandelier of the twelfth century, made for the Benedictine abbey at Comburg near Schwäbish-Hall. In the fourteenth century an important change took place in the construction of chandeliers, which became forerunners of new era chandeliers. Individual lighting bars or arms were suspended on a suspension pole, often with figural ornaments and sometimes several were found, one above the other. In the Gothic period, brass or bronze was widely used for these chandeliers, e.g. one in the town hall at Goslar from the fourteenth century or a chandelier in the parish church at Waase on the island of Rügen.

Very few medieval objects of copper have survived, and we tend to know their

56 Late Gothic bronze mortar with four ribs. Central Europe, second half of 15th century. Height 15.5 cm. Museum of the City of Prague.

the household and for craftsmen like soap-makers, tanners and wax-makers. The artisans produced pitchers, dishes, pots and crockery for daily use. Most of these articles were either made of wood or baked clay, and metal objects tended to be the exception and belonged exclusively to richer households. From what we know, the most important region for working copper was the lower Rhineland and the Maas valley, i.e. the traditional regions of metal works, where products were exported to the remotest parts of Europe. It is very difficult today to reconstruct the appearance of these objects of daily use because of a lack of surviving examples and the very sporadic interest of contemporary painters in such everyday utensils. Things of copper were easily damaged by regular use and — as we shall see — most of the older and used pieces were then turned into new articles. Throughout the Middle Ages and in later times, copper was used for roofing and as a suitable material for technical equipment, irrigation pipes and richly adorned and shaped gargoyles on churches and secular buildings. There are more reports that refer to the Gothic period and we can gain some kind of picture, though not precise, of what copper and brass-makers produced at that time. In the first place, large coppers which were used in every household. At least one such copper was kept on the stove to ensure a steady supply of hot water.

When the burghers went to the baths, so popular at the time, they would take along their own copper or brass tubs. For instance, Mistress Hester, the wife of a goldsmith, bequeathed to one of her relatives a copper tub that she had herself used when she went to the baths. Barbers, too, had their own special copper utensils. Written records frequently mention 'copper basins they took along for fish'. Such basins had a lid with a fish in relief on it. Then there were coppers for washing the laundry and copper utensils of various shapes and for different uses in the kitchen. Brass or copper tripods were placed under pots and pans by the fire. There were many domestic objects in households in the Middle Ages but because of the pottery of the times only a few were made of metal ware.

shapes and uses more from pictures. On the other hand, copper played an important role in the production of ecclesiastical objects, when it began to replace precious metals, which were in short supply in the early Middle Ages. Copper was used to make chalices, crosses, reliquaries, reliquary busts, candelabra, censers and other things. Easily shaped copper, which could be gilded, suited the goldsmiths and it proved a fitting base for various goldsmith's techniques, e.g. setting with brightly coloured enamels. Understandably, in such a situation copper objects began to conform to the art of the goldsmith in form and ornamentation. Such objects of copper were made in Italy and Germany, in Bohemia and France.

In the Middle Ages, the production of various objects of daily use also existed including various kettles and coppers for

The Renaissance Period

The fifteenth century was an important milestone in European history. The Renaissance originated in the south of Europe, in Italy, and as a style it gradually replaced Gothic art throughout the whole of Europe linked with a deliberate return to the art of Antiquity. The study of the literature and art of Greek and Roman culture led, eventually, to the rejection of Gothic art as both alien to Italy and barbarian in character. In Italy where Gothic art never sank the same deep roots as it did north of the Alps, this process advanced more speedily, starting in the early fifteenth century. In western, central and northern Europe the Renaissance style arrived and ended within one hundred years. In France Renaissance forms soon became a national style. In the Netherlands, Spain, Germany and in the whole

57 Two bronze taps in the shape of dolphins. Bohemia, 17th century. Length 40.5 and 32 cm. Museum of the City of Prague.

58 Bronze inkwell on three
feet with relief ornaments.
Italy, 16th century. Height
5.5 cm. Museum of
Decorative Arts, Prague.

Candlestick used in the 15th
century.

of Central Europe, its influence became
mixed with the local styles influenced by
the heritage of Late Gothic art.

The art of the Italian Renaissance was
born in Florence, and it soon turned into
a broad current that became the rebirth of
the art of Antiquity. For our theme it is
important that the renewed interest in
works of art of Antiquity led to the re-dis-
covery of bronze, the alloy of copper and
tin. The beautiful patina of the ancient
works of art was greatly admired. The
spread of metal-casting was conditioned
in Italy by the social setting in the country
and led once again to Italy gaining domi-
nance in this field throughout the fifteenth
and sixteenth centuries. A leading role
was played by small bronze sculptures,
which Italian Renaissance society began
to collect. These sculptures could instan-
taneously react to contemporary artistic,
literary and mental stimuli. The renewed

interest and public commissions played
a decisive role, making metal-casting an
art practised by the leading sculptors. To
select but a few of the entire cluster of artists we can mention Lorenzo Ghiberti
(1378—1455), Donatello (1386—1466)
and Andrea Riccio (c. 1470—1532).

Naturally, the high artistic and technical level of free-standing bronze sculpture
was reflected in objects that we today include in the applied arts. This somewhat
unfortunate division of art into fine and
applied was not true of the Renaissance
period, and so small inkwells, entire writing sets, vases and tall candelabras as well
as small transportable candlesticks were
decorated with sculpture, reliefs and ornamentation of high artistic quality. The
subjects were derived as in sculpture from
the ancient arts, particularly since these
superb small works were not intended for
ecclesiastical purposes. Mythological

59 Bronze votive candlestick of the Prague guild of maltsters. The Latin dedication is dated 1532. Made by Hans Vischer of Nuremberg. Height 240 cm. St Wenceslas Chapel in St Vitus' Cathedral, Prague. Photo SÚPPOP, Prague.

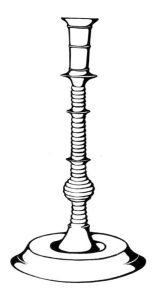

Candlestick used in the 15th century.

scenes and figures, lions, bulls, wolves and horses, amorettes and caryatids decorated objects of daily use or display in the home. There were even biblical scenes, allegories of the virtues and themes from Christian iconography.

By contrast to former periods these works are linked with the names of individual artists rather than production areas. This trend began at the Florentine court of the Medicis where artists ceased to be regarded as mere craftsmen belong-

60   Bronze door knocker in the shape of two figures of children, Medici emblem, mask of a satyr. Italy, 16th century. Diameter of the ring 25 cm. Museum of Decorative Arts, Prague.

61 Bronze door knocker in the shape of dolphins. The lower part has the form of a mascaroon. Italy, end of 16th century. Diameter 7.5 cm. Museum of Decorative Arts, Prague.

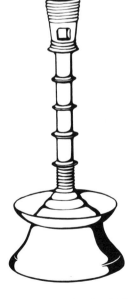

Candlestick used in the 15th century.

ing to the same category as shoemakers, coopers or tailors. They now ranked among the intellectuals, and society appreciated them as such. For that reason we can find Italian bronzes associated with the names of specific artists, e.g. the ornaments on the fountain in the Doges' Palace in Venice were made by Alfonso Alberghetti in the year 1559. A four-metre tall bronze candlestick in the Paduan basilica of San Antonio dates from the years 1507—16. It is the work of Andrea Riccio. The bronze pedestal to hold the Venetian flag on St Mark's Square is the

62 Detail of the ornaments
on the mortar on colour
photo No. 48.

Jug, before 1570.

work of sculptor and architect Alessandro Leopardi, who made it in the early sixteenth century.

In the countries north of the Alps the situation differed. Here the Renaissance had to counter the strong Gothic tradition. It was accepted with greater difficulty than in Italy since Antiquity was not regarded there as a period when cultural and political life flourished. Nonetheless, neither the north nor the west of Europe could resist the attraction of Renaissance ideas. Strangely enough, it was not Germany with its long tradition of metal-casting that held the leading position in this field. That was the privilege of artists from the Netherlands, who worked in many parts of Europe. Adriaen de Vries (probably 1560—1626), Alexander Colin (probably 1527—1612), Peter Candid de Witte (1548—1628), names that can be found in Germany as well as at the court of Rudolf II in Prague. Only the Nurem-

berg metal casting plant of the Vischer family could compete with these artists. The workshop was active from the middle of the fifteenth to the middle of the sixteenth century (1453—1554) and produced monumental works like fountains, tombstones and gravestones. The best known is the tomb of St Sebald in Nuremberg, made by Peter Vischer (1507—19). They also made small sculptures and objects of daily use. This workshop was of great significance in the German region since it advanced German Late Gothic Style towards the new Renaissance attitude. The Nuremberg plant of the Vischers was famous throughout Europe, and works made there can be found in many countries on the continent. Bronze became once again popular for large works. An example is the bronze tomb of Emperor Maximilian at Innsbruck, which, unfortunately, is unfinished because of the premature death of the Emperor. It was to have been decorated with more than 170 statues. Work on the tomb was carried out by a large number of artists, and Peter Vischer personally cast two of the statues in 1513.

The change in style can be traced on sanctuary rings. The formerly popular shape of the lion's head with large ring in its jaws, adopted from the art of Antiquity, was no longer found as frequently. When it did appear, its composition was not nearly as ecclesiastical as in the preceding period. The circular handle or knocker changed in shape too, becoming either oval or in the form of a lyre, and most were made of animal or even human figures. The lion's head was replaced by the head of a faun, a satyr or other creatures from ancient mythology. Very often the entire ring was covered with Renaissance relief ornaments. On such doorknockers the artist's phantasy knew few bounds so that Renaissance sanctuary rings can be found with the most varied shapes and ornaments, particularly so in Italy where the art of small sculpture reached a new height.

Apart from these purely artistic works,

63   Dish of hammered brass with the figure of a stag in the base. Nuremberg, 16th century. Diameter 32 cm. National Museum, Prague.

65 Bell with floral and figural decoration in relief. Engraved inscription 'S. Marcus, S. Matheus'. Italy, 16th century. Museum of Decorative Arts, Prague.

◁
64 Copper vessel (incense-burner?) with the figure of a frog on the lid. Engraved inscription 'Folbracht 11 May 1575'. Germany (?). Height 21 cm. National Museum, Prague.

bronze and brass were used to make articles of daily use. For example, bronze pots on three legs with a handle to stand or hang by the fireplace can be found. Their shape was known and tested in practical life so that there was little that needed changing. Another essential kitchen utensil made by the metal founder was the mortar, which underwent certain changes in form in the sixteenth century. While, in the most northerly regions of Europe, the mortar kept its Gothic verticality at that time, in the southern parts of the continent the sides of the mortar were more rounded, and it became shorter and wider. There were still relief ornaments and figural decorations, and the religious motifs were interspersed with Renaissance putti, allegories of the Muses, portraits, etc. The handle formed part of the ornament. Apart from those in the shape of horse's heads, dolphins enjoyed great popularity. This motif spread from Italy to the whole of Europe. It was popular not only on mortars but on other objects, mainly those associated with water, such as water spouts, fountains, water taps, etc. The popularity of the dolphin as an ornamental feature survived far into the seventeenth century and was revived in the Empire style in the early nineteenth century.

Kitchen utensils in Europe still included the three-legged cauldron in the sixteenth century. W. Dexel tried to classify these kitchen utensils according to types used in Germany and adjacent lands. He devised four basic types: those used in northern Germany called 'Grapen', at that time fairly flat and rather like a dish; the type used in the northwest, i.e. the Lower Rhineland and the Netherlands, with the characteristic drop shape. A third type was used in the southern zone, i.e. present day Austria, Bavaria, Swabia and the German-speaking parts of Switzerland. Here such three-legged caul-

66 Two small Renaissance brass candlesticks. Central Europe, second half of 16th century. Height 11.5 cm. Museum of Decorative Arts, Prague.

67   Bronze mortar with handles in the
shape of dolphins. Below the upper rim there
is the inscription 'LOF — GODT — VAN —
AL — A° — 1614'. Germany (?). Height
11 cm. Museum of Decorative Arts, Prague.

68 Tray on which stood Holy Communion
vessels in copper with remnants of silvering.
The inscription 'SUMPTIBUS P:
WENCESLAY ADALBERTY ZAPEK
DECANI POLNENSIS . . . 1681' is
engraved on the base. Bohemia.
22.5×28.7 cm. National Museum, Prague.

69   Copper lavabo. Engraved inscription
'FRANTZ PAUR 1706'. Hammered
decorations, tin-plated inside. Central
Europe. Height 16.2 cm. National Museum,
Prague.

70 Brass smoothing iron with relief
decorations and the inscription
'MARIA+FRANCISCA/TERESIA+
LÖWIN 1694'. Nuremberg (?). Length
18.5 cm. Museum of the City of Prague.

71   Bronze mortar. The outer side is
decorated with reliefs of the Crucifixion, The
Virgin and Child, angels heads and
a circular medallion with an equestrian
portrait of Emperor and King Ferdinand III.
Bohemia or Austria, first half of 17th
century. Height 15.5 cm. Museum of the
City of Prague.

72   Medallion on the mortar on colour photo No. 71. The equestrian portrait of Emperor and King Ferdinand III (1637—57). Wording: FERDINAND III D.G. RO. M.IM.

73 Copper and brass bottles with pewter caps. Central Europe, 18th century. Height of the tallest bottle 28.5 cm. Museum of the City of Prague.

74   Two typical 18th-century household
articles: a pot for fish and a bed-warmer with
an engraved coat-of-arms of a bishop on the
lid. Height of pot 25 cm, diameter of
bed-pan 28.5 cm. Museum of the City of
Prague.

drons were known as 'Glockenspeishaf-en', after the material of which they were made. They had two typical shapes: a rounded transition between neck and body of the vessel and one that Dexel called sack-shaped. Both these types were popular in the southern zone for many centuries and did not change in shape. There were also bronze pots not found in the north.

In the sixteenth century the standard of dwellings and household equipment among the richer members of the population improved. Many objects have survived, among them broad dish-shaped bronze vessels on a cylindrical base with rich Renaissance relief on the outside. It is assumed that, filled with water, they were used to keep wine cold. In the room of the master of the house there appeared writing sets and a bell, usually with a handle in the shape of a figure and relief ornaments on the outside, often with the coat-of-arms of the owner. They were used to call servants. Most of these table bells are made of a beautiful golden coloured alloy proving that a larger proportion of tin was used in the alloy to achieve a clear tone.

At the end of the fifteenth century and far into the seventeenth, Nuremberg held a similar privileged status as Dinant had done for brass production in the early Middle Ages. It is thought that after the destruction of Dinant in 1466 some of the brass-makers moved to Nuremberg where they laid the foundations of this craft. The oldest products from Nuremberg are dishes of brass plate with rich relief ornaments. It is very difficult to determine where individual pieces were made. They were produced in Nuremberg but also in other towns and were exported to the whole of Europe. As M. Wiswe pointed out other production centres existed, e.g. in Brunswick; Lübeck recorded fourteen master dish-embossers in 1330. In the

75 Late Renaissance brass candlestick from the turn of the 16th to 17th century. Central Europe. Height 42 cm. Museum of the City of Prague.

German lands their popularity declined rapidly in the seventeenth century except in the southern regions, while in the Netherlands and in Sweden production remained at a remarkable level long into the eighteenth century.

Other craftsmen used sheet brass for their products too, particularly those who made small objects for use or decoration. Such articles were exported to the whole of Europe.

One of the specialities of the Nuremberg braziers was the production of nests of weights. Some have interesting figural ornaments. The weights were marked with a compulsory letter 'N' from 1538 on. Apart from this letter, the producers of scales and weights also used the mark of a trefoil until the nineteenth century. The special position of the Nuremberg producers of weights came to an end in the 1730s. In 1738 a state weights factory was set up in Prussia, in Potsdam, which had a swan as its mark, and another began work in Berlin in 1766. Other states seem to have taken similar measures (W. Stengel).

During this period copper objects were a great rarity. Very few can be definitively attributed to the sixteenth century. The reason must be that old, broken or no longer fashionable copper objects were either handed over by the owner to the metal-caster in part payment for a new object, or they were bought by founders or hammer-mill owners who, as we shall see in the chapter on the technology of production, used them for new melts, bronze or copper. One of the few objects with a date that has survived is a copper pot, perhaps a censer, now in the National Museum in Prague. It bears the inscription 'Folbracht 11 May 1575'.

In the Renaissance period the mining of copper ore increased in Europe with the discovery of new deposits in the Ore

76 Bronze trivet with a wooden handle. The actual base composed of S-shaped ornament and conical pillars grows out of the supporting legs on which the year 1668 is engraved. The handle ends in the figure of Atlas supporting the globe. England, 1668. Length 58.4 cm. Victoria and Albert Museum, London.

77 Brass candlestick from the early 16th century. Probably German. Height 17.5 cm. Museum of Decorative Arts, Prague.

Mountains of Bohemia. In the first place these were silver ore mines which, especially at Jáchymov (1516), led to a silver rush, but deposits of non-ferrous metals, such as copper, tin, lead and zinc, were also found.

In the early sixteenth century mining technology was improved with a number of new inventions and the perfection of existing machinery.

In the first place there was the pump to draw water out of the mines. Ventilation equipment was improved, as was hoisting machinery and mine transportation by the introduction of waggons all of which raised the productivity of labour. Understandably, all this modernization was costly. These costs were taken on by rich business houses, such as the Fuggers of Augsburg, who, in the first half of the sixteenth century, were Europe's main financiers. In the years 1495—1526 they partly financed the Banská Bystrica Copper Company in Upper Hungary, which owned mines, foundries, forges, stores and other premises. The Fuggers at first shared the costs with another mining entrepreneur, Jan Thurzo. But in 1526—46 the Fuggers were the sole owners of the Company. After 1546 this company passed into the hands of the Austrian state and was administered by it until mining ceased in 1888. Mining reached its peak in the sixteenth century.

The Fuggers also tried to participate in copper mining in England. Queen Elizabeth supported local production of copper and its alloys for economic and military reasons since brass and bronze products, mostly firearms, were, to a large extent, imported from the Continent. The Company 'Mercatores de Dinant in Alemania' held trade firmly in its hands and under its control. From 1564 the Fuggers were represented in negotiations with the Queen by Hang and Co. Another German, Daniel Hochstetter, managed to found the 'Mines Royal Societie' in 1568, which, from 1571 on, built mines at Keswick employing 400 miners summoned from Germany.

Another mining enterprise in England was set up by a man from the country with a rich tradition, by J. Schultz from Saxony, who, with William Humphrey, an Assay Master of the Mint, founded the Society of the Mineral and Battery Mines in 1568. They mined calamine in the Mendip Hills in Somerset. The two companies were not greatly successful. Copper merchants still preferred suppliers on the Continent, and the Mineral and Battery Society had major problems with the quality of the brass they produced. In addition, the two companies were affected by events in the Civil War. British copper, as an industry, did not flourish properly until the eighteenth century.

The Baroque Period

Baroque art is a term that embraces various currents in art. What appeared to the observer living at the time as an entity we today regard as full of artistic contradictions.

The applied arts, and with them works made of bronze, brass or copper, very sensitively followed all these develop-

ments in style. To understand these changes it is necessary to sum up briefly the historical background and the differences within this art form, which dominated Europe for two centuries. Far be it for us to attempt to find a solution to these theoretical disputes.

Two countries, Italy and France, became the art centres of the time, and both spread their ideas on art throughout the Continent. The development of Baroque art in Italy took place against the historical background of the struggle of the Catholic Church against the Reformation in the North, which broke up the existing unity of the Christian world. In this world of ideological struggles the Catholic Church conceived art as a valuable ally against the endeavours of the Reformation. Papal Rome took a lead in supporting art. Its immense effort to rebuild the Eternal City into an ostentatious residence of the Head of the Church set an example to the Catholic aristocracy and the courts of princes. This need for display so typical of Baroque society was employed to an unheard-of extent in all spheres of the arts. The main role was assumed by architecture, which involved the co-operation of all other branches of the arts and came to dominate them. Architecture shows best that there was no formal unity in European Baroque art. On the contrary, two contradictory principles of art clashed: the dynamic principle, which expressed all its artistic aims by movement of form and space without regard to the laws of nature, and Neo-Classicism, which never abandoned the heritage of the Renaissance, the example of Antiquity being its binding directive. Competition between these two trends in style continued throughout the seventeenth and eighteenth centuries. Neo-Classicism proved victorious at the end of the Baroque

78   Bronze mortar with two handles in the form of spikes. Central Europe, 17th century. Height 9 cm. Museum of Decorative Arts, Prague.

101

79 Three examples of Baroque candlesticks. On the left, the candlestick with the hectagonal base and relief heads of little angels on the drip tray dates from the 17th century. In the centre the candlestick from the 18th century is decorated with twisted fluting. The candlestick on the right has a propped stem and a wide flat base. Height of the left candlestick 28.5 cm. Museum of the City of Prague.

epoch since the radical current had exhausted all its creative possibilities, but by that time the entire creative climate in Europe had changed.

Baroque art spread from its country of birth, Italy, to the whole of Europe but affected different branches of the arts with varying intensity. The two main principles, Neo-Classicism and the dynamic principle, found varying responses in individual countries. While Neo-Classicism dominated the field in France and England, the dynamic trend found followers mainly in Central Europe and on the Iberian Peninsula. Furthermore, these tendencies were coloured by specific local features so that Baroque art disintegrated into many patterns or trends.

Bronze-casting and brass and copper working succumbed to the unifying strength of Baroque art and followed its creative trend in the way explained in the preceding paragraphs. Works of art and simple objects for daily use followed the contemporary view that all works, ranging from architecture to door-handles, should be in harmony to kindle an edifying and unforgettable enjoyment of art. The strength of Baroque ideas and style spread to the day-to-day life of townspeople and rural folk. Baroque ornamental features can be found on vernacular architecture and on folk costume and even on horse harness, and this continued far into the nineteenth century.

The need for official involvement in the rebuilding of Rome into a modern city is reflected also in bronze-making. Two works were made for St Peter's cathedral, the central sanctuary of the Catholic

80 Water holder made from sheet copper and engraved with flowers and the letters 'T. A. F. Anno 1705'. Height 25 cm. Pinkas Synagogue, State Jewish Museum, Prague.

Two types of bronze trivets for the open hearth with attachments for a wooden handle, before 1570.

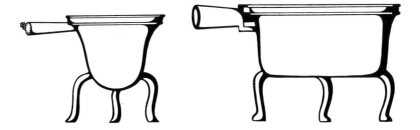

81 Two flint-and-steel clocks with a lighting mechanism. The clockwork case is made of gilded brass popular among clock-makers.
The clock is signed 'Ferdinant Engelschalck/ Prag' and 'Johan Maurer/Prag'. Engelschalck's workshop is recorded in Prague for the years 1705—52, Maurer's from 1725—31. The size of the clocks is almost identical, 17×9×5.5 cm. Museum of the City of Prague.

Design for a three-sided tap. Drawing in a Bohemian manuscript, before 1570.

Church. In size and conception they exceeded all that had ever been made of bronze. One is the famous bronze canopy above the Papal Altar located over the tomb of St Peter. It is the work of Gian Lorenzo Bernini, that genius of Italian Baroque sculptors and architects who won fame with this monumental, 29-metres high, masterpiece. Bernini added to the interior furnishings of the church the

majestic Throne of St Peter, made in the years 1657—66 on the order of Pope Alexander VII. Four figures of the Church Fathers stand on a marble pedestal bearing a bronze throne, in which the ancient wooden chair is set which St Peter is alleged to have used. Both masterpieces are examples of the technical skill of Baroque metal-casters who knew no limits to casting bronze.

As demands in art changed the small bronze objects that had been so popular in Renaissance Italy lost admirers. All efforts of the time turned to larger works, which could be admired in public. The small bronze works of the Renaissance had been intended only for the private cabinets of collectors. Something did survive of the perfection of the small Renaissance bronzes: the door-knockers to which artists continued to devote attention. Figural ornaments vanished on Baroque door-knocker, but ornaments were created according to the laws of dynamics

Bronze kitchen utensil, before 1570.

82 Dial and case with the signature of the maker of the alarm and lighting mechanism of the flint-and-steel clock in picture 81.

with the most varied shapes in agile movement. In the seventeenth century the centre of work in bronze and brass moved to France. Here the high demand on art, set by the French royal court and the upper nobility, provided a suitable climate for creative work. This gave rise to another art centre whose example influenced a broad sphere of European countries.

While the moving force of art in Italy was the papal court, in France this role was assumed for two whole centuries by the Monarchy. Both Louis XIV (1643—1715) and Louis XV (1723—74) and even Louis XVI (1774—93) personally influenced art in the whole of France. This decisive influence of the monarch on all spheres of the arts led to the unheard of concentration of artists in the Académie Royale de Peinture et de Sculpture, founded in Paris on a proposal by Ch. Le Brun in 1648. Similarly craftsmen of all spheres were associated in the manufacture of furniture for the crown, where, in their work, they followed unified designs as supplied chiefly from the royal cus-

tomer. Naturally, French art underwent some development even in this specific situation. Individual periods are, therefore, called by the names of the ruling monarch. 'Louis XIV' is a typical style of official art following a restrained Neo-Classical order, while 'Louis XV' brought relaxation. Its typical feature was rocaille so that sometimes it is known as 'Flamboyant Baroque' as well as the general term of Rococo. But after 1750 opposition arose to the rocaille style and so the subsequent phase of 'Louis XVI' marked the transition from Rococo to Neo-Classicism.

The applied arts followed all these trends, chiefly in ornamentation and interior furnishings. The more refined way of life brought new demands for the setting in which people lived. Naturally bronze, brass and copper with their varied colours found full application. By coincidence perhaps the most interesting achievement in bronze and brass was in furniture-making, the work of specialized cabinet-makers, called 'ebenists' in

83 Copper pot on three iron legs with an iron handle. Hammered inscription 'M. C. Lara 1738'. Southern Germany (?). Height 32.5 cm. Museum of the City of Prague.

France. As the name shows, these cabinet-makers, first mentioned in 1657 as 'menuisiers en ébène', originally worked the valuable ebony wood of tropical origin and later they made all manner of luxury furniture. It was their task to harmonize the work of all specialists, including that of bronze-casters and sculptors, to create a masterpiece. The most famous ebenist under Louis XIV was André Charles Boulle (1642—1732), who decorated veneer furniture with ornamental marquetry composed of various materials, especially tortoise-shell and brass, often with gilded engravings. Brass played a very important role here in providing a colour contrast to the darker tortoise-shell. Brass as an ornament was used in two ways: as 'premier effet à partie' or 'boulle', i.e. an ornament in light coloured brass on the darker base of tortoise-shell (positive intarsia), and as 'deuxième effet' or 'contre-boulle', i.e. an ornament of tortoise-shell against the lighter background of brass (negative intarsia).

In France the ebenists were regarded as artists and were expected to satisfy demands. Furniture decorated in this exacting technique was highly vulnerable, especially where the edges of the inlaid wood met. This danger led to the protection of the edges with bronze or brass, replacing the simple outline of carved furniture and strengthening the entire construction. Gradually the bronze parts became appreciated as ornaments on the furniture, especially in the period of Louis XV. They protected the precious inlay, gave stress to the construction and outline, emphasized the curves and formed the ends of the legs of the furniture. A famous ebenist of this phase was Jean François Oeben, who became the King's purveyor in 1754. His workshop made the 'bureau du roi', a writing desk for Louis XV, a true masterpiece. Work on it was begun in 1760, and it took a full nine years. In 1763 Oeben died so that his successor, J. H. Riesener, took over the completion of the bureau. This work cost nearly one million francs, paid out of the royal treasury. Gold marquetry was used for the ornamentation.

J. F. Oeben invited specialists to create the bronze decorations that made use of every colour combination of this noble alloy. The design and models were prepared by Claude Thomas Chambellan,

106

84   Jug of sheet copper. At the front a hammered maltsters' emblem (two crossed maltsters' tools) between two walking lions. The year 1747 is hammered on the lid. Bohemia. Height 34 cm. Museum of the City of Prague.

called Duplessis, the director of the workshop for designing and fitting bronze in the porcelain manufacture at Vincennes à Sèvres. Louis Barthélemy Hervieu was entrusted with the task of casting and chasing. He was an outstanding craftsman who, among others, made the gilded bronze ornaments in the Lady Chapel of the church of Saint-Sulpice in Paris, finished in c. 1777. Other outstanding bronze-casters and chasers worked for J. F. Oeben, namely Etienne Forestier (c. 1712—68) and Philippe Caffieri the Younger (1714—74). They were members of family workshops that profoundly influenced the artistic and technical level of casting and chasing bronze in France. Works by Forestiers, both father Etienne and son, Etienne Jean, were highly prized, particularly that of brother Pierre Auguste (1755—1838), who supplied outstanding works to the court of Louis XVI.

The Caffieri family was of basic import-ance for the production of artistic bronzes in France. The founder, Philippe Caffieri the Elder, born in Rome 1634, was summoned to Paris by Cardinal Giulio Mazarini in 1660. He was primarily an interior decorator, and as an artist, participated in the interior decorations of the châteaux at Marly, the Tuileries, the Louvre and Versailles. His son, Jacques Caffieri (1678—1755), was a brazier and sculptor and worked mainly on commissions for the king; among outstanding works by him are clock decorations, which the clockmaker and constructor of astronomical instruments, Claude-Simon Passemant (1702—69), made for Louis XV in 1753. His exceptional feeling for bronze can be exemplified on many other works, today scattered in world-famous collections. The Wallace Collection in London owns a chest-of-drawers with rich bronze ornaments and a candelabrum and the Victoria and Albert Mu-

85 Tub hammered of sheet copper. A similar emblem of the maltsters as on jug in picture No. 84 is depicted on the body of the tub. Two iron handles. Bohemia, mid 18th century. Upper diameter 30 cm. Museum of the City of Prague.

86 Copper box with lid, brass mounts, with an iron handle on the lid. Austria, 17th century. Height 27 cm. Museum of the City of Prague.

seum has a writing desk belonging once to Prince Metternich in Vienna. His son, Philippe Caffieri the Younger (1714 to 1774), often collaborated with the ebenist J. F. Oeben. His main work concerned bronze home fittings, lamps and writing desks, various cupboards, sofas and fire-place ornaments. He also made bronze decorations and furniture parts. Amongst the many remarkable examples are his bronze mounts on a commode for the royal chambers at Versailles, made by A. R. Gaudreaux in 1739 to a design by the Slodtz Brothers. P. Caffieri junior was a representative of the Louis XV style, even though his works, in some ways, anticipated the calmer lines of Neo-Classicism.

Another outstanding bronze chaser was Pierre Gouthière (1732—1813/14), likewise a skilled gilder and draughtsman. The Master began work in 1758 and was soon given important commissions. The third quarter of the eighteenth century

87 Copper jug with a rim for it to be set in
a hole in the stove-top. Central Europe, end
of 18th century. Height 35 cm. National
Museum, Prague.

witnessed the culmination of his work. He was then working for Madame Du Barry as her full-time bronze chaser, employed in decorating the château of Louveciennes near Marly. Another of his customers was the Prince of Aumont. Several objects have survived from that time, for example, a jasper vase set in a bronze tripod and two vases of serpentine with a wealth of bronze fittings, in-

cluding female figures and ram heads, now in the Louvre. One of his major works is the Avignon Clock of 1771, now in the Wallace Collection in London. The design was supplied by sculptor Louis Simon Boizot (1743 — 1809), the head of the porcelain works at Sèvres. The centre motif is the allegorical figure of Victory, holding the coat-of-arms of the Marquise de Rochechouart, and two re-

88 Brass candlestick with four branches for use on the Jewish Sabbath. An eagle at top centre. Eastern Europe, *c.* mid 18th century. Height 45.5 cm. State Jewish Museum, Prague.

89 Bronze andirons of a man and woman with cock and hen tails. Signed 'Caffieri fecit' (Jacques Caffieri). France, first half of 18th century. Musée des Arts Décoratifs, Paris.

clining female figures, who are the personifications of rivers. The Avignon Clock is the only signed work by P. Gouthière. For that reason the chief criterion for identifying Gouthière's work is the perfection of chasing on a given object. Pierre Gouthière had already been regarded a first-class artist, no wonder then that his co-operation was sought by the leading artists of the time, such as L. S. Boizot, Ch. M. A. Challe, C. M. Clodion, J. H. Riesener and J. A. Houdon. Some scholars think Gouthière invented matte gilding.

His pupil, Pièrre Philippe Thomire (1751—1843), achieved almost the same perfection in working bronze. In 1776 Thomire set up his own workshop, and in 1785 he became the official bronze worker of the porcelain works at Sèvres. A jewel-box for Marie Antoinette dates from 1787; it was made to a design by Percier. The work that brought Thomire greatest fame was made in the period after

1800, when the Empire style prevailed.

The list of excellent French bronze founders and chasers is far longer. One that should be mentioned is Etienne Martincourt, sculptor, bronze-caster and chaser, and from 1763, Assistant Professor at the Academy Saint-Luc. Two interesting candlesticks made by him are today in the Wallace Collection in London. Another was bronze-maker, Feuchères, who worked for Marie Antoinette and in 1788 he made a set of two three-armed candlesticks for her toilet cabinet, which are decorated with quivers and doves. As late as 1812 he had made two candlesticks with figures of children for the imperial chambers.

The Paris bronze founders were organized in the 'fondeurs-ciseleurs' guild and jealously guarded their privileges, particularly those that concerned the production of bronze ornaments and furniture fittings. For that reason furniture-makers bought bronze ornaments from the guild

90   a/ Copper chalice with hammered and engraved decorations. It is decorated with (1) the coat-of-arms of the guild of butchers (the Bohemian lion with a hatchet in the front paws); (2) coat-of-arms of the Old Town of Prague; (3) the inscription '1700 / Johhan Kletezka / 1750'. The letters S.R.J.B.W.Z.K. are hammered along the upper rim of the cup, on the stem the letters M/J/K. Prague. Height 18.2 cm.

b/ Copper chalice with S-shaped hammered ribs and an inscription around the upper edge of the cup: 'DAVID.BEN.ABR.OPPENHEIMER 1720'. Prague (?). Height 16.5 cm.
Both chalices are the property of the Museum of the City of Prague.

113

91 Bronze holy water font
with relief ornaments of
heads of angels. Gilded. At
the back the year 1758 is
engraved. Austria or
southern Germany. Height
of back wall 22 cm. Museum
of Decorative Arts, Prague.

92   Set of tobacco boxes of brass and
copper sheet. These boxes with repoussé
relief are marked in the decoration: 'GIESE
/ ISERLOHN'. The tobacco grater is
decorated with perforated ornament
including the coat-of-arms of the maltsters,
the letters ASS and the year 1762. The
tobacco box on the right is signed 'HAMER
FEC ISERLOHN'. Length 15 cm. Museum
of the City of Prague and private collection,
Prague.

93   Brass weights 32 lbs and 8 lbs.
Nuremberg, second half of 18th century.
Height of the largest weight 29.3 cm.
National Museum, Prague.

94   Detail of one of the weights on colour
photo No. 93.

95   View of Prague. Part of the decoration
on the tobacco box on colour photo No. 92.

118

96 Articles of copper made at Špania Dolina, Slovakia, 17th — 19th century. Museum of Decorative Arts, Prague.

97 Copper jug with the hammered figure of a lion on the lid. The year 1762 is engraved on the lid. Height 34 cm. Museum of the City of Prague.

masters, with the exception of the ebenists working for the king, for whom there were no guild restrictions. The renowned cabinet-maker and carver, Charles Cressent (1685—1768), a pupil of A. C. Boulle, had an unpleasant dispute with the bronze-makers' guild. The founders sued him for making his own bronze decorations for his furniture, though the law did not permit double employment. Official steps were taken against him, and the tools of his trade were confiscated as well as finished casts.

The high level of French art of this period was known all over Europe. The influence of French Rococo left a particularly strong mark on the court of Frederick the Great of Prussia. In the 1840s work began on furnishing the rooms of the royal palaces at Potsdam, Sanssouci and Charlottenburg. Johann August Nahl (1710 to 1785), one of Schlüter's disciples in Paris, was summoned to Berlin as 'directeur des ornements'. He collaborated with the Hoppenhaupt Brothers as carver and engraver J.W. Meil. Nahl, the Hoppenhaupts and Meil created a special North German Rococo, sometimes known as

98   Commode in the royal bedroom at Versailles. To a design by court artist S. A. Slodtz made by ebenist A. R. Gaudreau, gilt bronze decorations by Jacques Caffieri. Paris, 1739. Wallace Collection, London.

'Frederick or Prussian Rococo'. They copied in particular the French manner of making decorations of silvered or gilded bronze with the addition of mother-of-pearl, tortoise-shell or ivory.

Such major new constructions made great demands on interior decorations. As a consequence Johann Melchior Kambli (1718—83), a sculptor, cabinet-maker and first of all specialist at gilding or silvering bronze objects in the fire, obtained the king's permission to set up a 'Fabrique von bronze doré Arbeit' at Potsdam. One of the major works of this manufacture was the 'Bronzesaal' (Bronze Hall) in the Potsdam palace. The Rococo decorations of this hall, made chiefly of bronze gilded in the fire, were created to a design by J. A. Nahl in the years 1754—55. Records show that the gilding was the work of Morel, and that the chaser was Geoffroy. The latter's name confirms the report that in 1751 the workshop hired bronze-makers in Paris. The production of Kambli's workshop included other objects for interior decora-

99   Foot-warmer of sheet brass, octagonal. Hammered inscription 'Nicolas Schmuck Anno 1753'. Germany. Height 9.5 cm. Museum of Decorative Arts, Prague.

100 Wine cooler in sheet
copper with hammered
ornament. Two iron handles.
Central Europe, *c.* mid 18th
century. Largest diameter
55 cm. Museum of the City
of Prague.

tions, such as mirror frames, table and
wall candlesticks and clock cases. An important part of their work was the production of bronze furniture fittings supplied
to cabinet-makers. The leading cabinet-
makers of Prussian Rococo, who made
widespread use of the bronze decorations
from the Kambli workshop, were the
brothers Heinrich Wilhelm and Johann
Friedrich Spindler. They came to Potsdam
in 1764 and Johann Friedrich set up
manufacture there. Heinrich Wilhelm
then settled in Berlin. They were both
still working in 1799. It is difficult to
distinguish the work of the two makers
since the brothers often worked together.
Their chests-of-drawers, cupboards, writing and games tables, etc. are often over-
loaded with bronze decorations, mainly
in the form of flower vases or pendants
with figural motifs in a shell-shaped
frame. This is typical of Potsdam Rococo.

Mention should also be made of the
work of other German cabinet-makers:
the Röntgens. Father Abraham set up
manufacture at Neuwied in 1750. In his
work he tended to follow Dutch or English patterns, while his son David began,
after 1780, to substitute for the intarsia
heavy bronzes typical of Parisian work.
This may have been connected with their
opening a trading store of the Neuwied
factory in Paris that year. Around 1789
the workshop reached its peak producing
all kinds of furniture. David Röntgen died
in 1807.

In England furniture did not play as important a role as in France. While, on the
Continent, they placed emphasis on luxurious court furniture, in England they appreciated technical perfection rather than
ostentatious form. As a consequence,
brass furniture fittings tended to be restrained. Terse elegant lines with Neo-

123

124

102 Copper jug decorated
on the lower part with an
S-shaped hammered
ornamentation. Similar
decoration is found on the
lid. The spout is oblong in
shape. Iron handle. Central
Europe, before mid 18th
century. Height including lid
45 cm. Museum of the City
of Prague.

◁
101 Brass was highly
suitable for the production
of various instruments. The
equatorial sun-dial depicted
is signed 'Franciscus Merl
fecit Pragae A:1735'. Height
21 cm, diameter of the
round plate 17.5 cm.
Museum of the City of
Prague.

104 Andirons of gilt
bronze with figures of
Chinese men and women
from Bellevue château.
Louis XV style. Musée
National du Louvre, Paris.

◁

103 Painting by an
anonymous painter showing
the birth of John the Baptist.
It renders proof that the
original function of the
copper tub for cooling
beverages was lost by the
end of the 18th century.
Private collection, Prague.

Classical articulation of the walls and
similar trends in interior furnishing gave
English rooms a unique character. One
of the main artists of English Neo-Classi-
cial art was architect Robert Adam
(1728—92), whose book on Diocletian's
Palace, published in 1764, is regarded as
the basic work of the Classical Revival.
Adam's views on art left a profound mark
on all spheres of the decorative arts, including products of bronze, brass and
copper, and became known as the Adam
style.

Though the British bronze-founders
and chasers did not enjoy as much respect
as those in France, the production of
bronze, brass and copper was highly successful in Britain. It could look back on
a long tradition. We have a report from
the early seventeenth century, from 1603,
that there was one street in London where
metal-founders lived, who produced various objects such as buckles, candlesticks, mortars, alewarmers, etc. The brass-
makers in London were organized in the
Company of Braziers, which in 1708
merged with a similar guild, the Company

of Armourers. The bronze founders had
a laverpot in the coat-of-arms, which can
be seen in that of the Worshipful Company of Founders of London. The English
braziers were also organized in guilds in
other towns. A typical product made by
their skilful craftsmen in the seventeenth
century was the trivet, sometimes called
'footman'. Our examples date from 1668.
These trivets were used as stands for pots
or pans kept close to the fireplace. This
trivet is in exceptionally good condition
and is richly adorned with figural and ornamental motifs. As G. Wills wrote, the
British brass industry began to develop
rapidly in the early eighteenth century. It
began in the vicinity of Bristol where suitable conditions existed. Rich calamine deposits in the Mendip Hills, coal in the
Radstock district, copper in Cornwall
and, by no means least, cheap, readily
available water power from the rivers of
northern Somerset. In 1702 the Bristol
Brass Wire Company was established to
supply local needs and to export products
to the Continent and as far as Africa.

Before long, a dangerous competitor

105 Table alarm-clock. A hexagonal case of gilded bronze mounted in silver on three shaped legs. Enamel dial. Signed 'Johann Engelschalk in Prag'. The work of J. Engelschalk is recorded in Prague for the years 1754—74. Diameter 9.5 cm. Museum of the City of Prague.

chiefly abroad. Mr. Boulton told me that they now have very great influence at the Russian Court . . . and they hoped to supplant the French in the Gilt business.' Boulton produced furniture fittings on the French pattern and even made bronze mounts, for example candlesticks where the stem is made of a special kind of colourful stone, Derbyshire Spar, found near Castle on. Some scholars think that the British firms sent their products, especially furniture fittings, to France in a crude state where they were chased by French specialists. The scope of production in Birmingham is shown by a report from the year 1777. Thirty braziers annually used 1,000 tons of brass. They acquired zinc from Bristol where William Champion produced some 200 tons annually in 1740 (G. Savage).

After the Thirty Years' War, France became a leader in the arts. The rest of Europe followed the French pattern only in the eighteenth century when they overcame the consequences of the Thirty Years' War. In the Rococo period especially, the European ruling dynasties copied the French way of life with more or less success. Our attention is centred on utilitarian objects, which did not reap the admiration of experts of the time but, from the viewpoint of a present-day observer, are valuable witnesses to their age, and whose shapes and materials rouse our admiration.

In the first place, it should be noted that bronze vessels gave way to pots made of sheet copper. The production of such objects of copper can be traced from the seventeenth century in the countries north of the Alps, from Hungary and Austria to Bohemia, from there to Switzerland, the lower reaches of the Rhine to Holland and the coastal regions of northern Germany. Copper objects are far more longlasting than vessels made of wood or pottery. They are also lighter in weight and therefore easier to handle and as suitable for the fireplace as cast bronze or brass. By tin-plating the inside of the pots they became safe for use and the reddish colour of polished copper became a decoration in every kitchen. Compared with tin, copper had the advantage of greater resistance to heat and a harder surface and so, together with pewter, copper was widely used in the household during the seventeenth and eighteenth centuries. In

appeared in Birmingham, until that time known as the centre of steel products even though the brass founders in Birmingham can be traced back to 1689. In 1750 the Birmingham craftsmen and entrepreneurs began to pay increased attention to brass, and, before long, they came to dominate the British and foreign markets in brass products. As time passed, these became world famous. One of the leading Birmingham firms was Boulton and Fothergill. The factory was set up by Matthew Boulton (1728—1809) in 1762 when he enlarged his father's small workshop. G. Savage has published a letter from J. Wedgwood, who visited Boulton's factory in 1776. He reported to his partner, Bentley, the success and aspirations of the factory: 'I had no conception of the quantity of D'Or Moulu they have sold,

106 The writing desk of Louis XV. Work on the table was begun by the ebenist J. F. Oeben in 1760 and after his death the desk was finished by J. H. Riesener in 1769. The gilt bronze ornaments on the desk were modelled by Duplessis, cast and chased by L. Hervieu. Signed 'Riesener H. f., 1769 à l'Arsenal de Paris'. Musée National du Château de Versailles.

the second half of the nineteenth century, copper was displaced from its sovereign position by new materials of similar quality but cheaper and therefore suitable for mass production.

During the seventeenth and eighteenth centuries there were vessels of every type and kind all suited to the requirements of everyday life and made with considerable craftsmanship. The artisans of the time show great skill and a fine feeling for the material itself. For present-day collectors it is difficult to determine the provenance of certain objects, with some exceptions, because copper was exported from production centres to the whole of Europe.

Basic household equipment included cooking pots. With the changeover from an open fireplace to an enclosed cooking range with iron plates — a transition that in different places occurred at different times — there emerged a new type of receptacle, the cooking-pan. The existing vessel on three legs with a mighty handle for suspension and intended to be used on the open fire had mostly been cast in bronze and it now went out of use. The new pan had a flat bottom, two handles for easier manipulation and sometimes even a spout along the upper edge. Pans of different size were some of the least complicated household utensils in shape.

107 Brass lamp decorated with two relief lions holding the portrait of the Austrian Emperor Joseph II. Bohemia, *c.* 1785. Width 28.5 cm. State Jewish Museum, Prague.

This was not so in the case of kettles, where the craftsman had to follow regional peculiarities. It is, therefore, easier to determine, roughly at least, from which regions of Europe such kettles originated. In Central Europe, for instance, kettles of pear shape were popular, with a broad S-shaped handle on the side and usually with a hinged lid. Kettles with a broad, round body, sometimes on three legs and, of course, with handle and spout came from the regions of northern Europe. A receptacle with a cone-shaped body and handle was used all over Europe to hold water. At the end of the eighteenth and in the first half of the nineteenth century, jars with a lid and spring catch were in great demand. Most of them were conical, but there are even barrel-shaped receptacles of this kind. An interesting fea-

ture of the Swiss region were 'Brunnenkesselchen', made in large numbers of copper and tin. With a movable handle and pipe-shaped spout below the upper edge they were hung in rooms or dining rooms above the wash-basin and were ready for washing hands.

Another liquid container widespread throughout Europe was a bottle or flask with a screw-top, mostly made of pewter. Such bottles are of varied shape, while those made of copper are mostly cylindrical, sometimes double-walled, and nearly always with embossed or engraved ornament according to the taste of the time. Some have inscriptions and dates.

At the end of the seventeenth and early eighteenth century, two new beverages rapidly became popular in Europe — tea and coffee. Both these exotic novelties brought with them the need for special receptacles in which the drinks could be prepared or served at table. Tea came to Europe from China in two ways. It was brought by ship by Dutch and French merchants and overland by caravans passing through Russia. The European merchants brought not only tea but also the special Chinese pots used for the beverage — the pottery or porcelain teapots, which became the pattern for European products. In Europe the teapots were made of a variety of materials, mainly of porcelain or often of silver, but they were also made of copper, and their basic shape has virtually remained unchanged to this day.

The origin of the coffee-jug is not as clear as that of the teapot. Such relatively tall jugs of S-shaped outline with a handle and spout were not known in Europe before the arrival of coffee. With use, this type of coffee-jug became generally accepted in the first half of the eighteenth century, and it remains popular even today.

Though these two types of receptacles were produced of varying materials such as pottery, porcelain, pewter or silver, we

108 Copper container in which hot embers were kept overnight in the Netherlands, where these were called 'Doovpötte'; brass lid and handle. End of 18th century. Height 34 cm. Private collection, Prague.

131

can also find attractive examples made of copper. Most of them are quite smooth, without embossed or engraved ornament, and they are attractive for their refined shape and smooth, reddish surface rubbed to a high polish.

Present-day research has not advanced enough to make it possible to describe all types of liquid receptacles, their regional or local peculiarities or their spread to various parts of Europe. Generally, valid conclusions will be drawn only after more detailed investigations even though increased attention has been given to these matters in specialist publications.

109 Detail of the dish on colour photo No. 96.

Copper was not just used for vessels to hold liquids. Kitchen utensils included salt-boxes to be hung on the wall. The back and the actual container for the salt were almost always decorated with embossed or engraved ornaments, often based on local folklore.

In the household an important place was reserved for warming-pans, a vessel of circular shape with a lid on a long wooden or metal handle. It was filled with hot charcoal, and the lid had holes in it so that air would keep the charcoal burning. This type of warming-pan was used to heat the beds before bedtime. The pan was moved across the sheets like a large smoothing iron. The lid of the pan was often decorated with embossed or engraved ornaments, following period taste, often with figural or animal motifs and quite often with inscripions.

In southern Europe, and also in the central parts of the Continent, tub-shaped vessels were highly popular from the end of the seventeenth century. They had two moveable handles for transportation and were originally used to cool wine or other beverages, as shown by numerous period illustrations. These pots were probably in wide use, the surviving numbers show their great popularity and even today they are used as decorative jardinières.

In some parts of Europe copper containers for special use have survived. In Saxony there existed large bread-boxes, sometimes up to one metre high with a lid and two handles for easier shifting. On these, too, the walls and the lid were decorated. Dutch 'Doovpöte' were used to keep coals hot overnight. Copper was a popular material for such pots as well as pottery. Most of them were circular with a smooth cone-shaped body, and the walls are slightly concave. The legs, lid and handle were often made of brass, which led to an interesting colour effect, combining the reddish copper with the goldenish colour of brass.

Other interesting receptacles were large copper grape carriers identical in shape with the classical wooden ones. They were richly adorned with engraved and relief ornaments, which were usually centred on the tall back of the tub that protected the back of the carrier.

Remarkable objects of copper plate also included German apothecary's jars, cylindrical in shape and widening towards

110 Tankard with gilded copper lid. On the lid there is a small figure of a miner. On the medallion on the vessel the inscription is engraved on a gilt background: 'Gott / lass einkehren aller orten / Gold Silber und Kupfer / sorten, zu Kremnitz Schem / nitz und Neüsohl, gera / the Gold Silber und Kupfer wohl'. On the rim: 'Gott beschere alles mild was ich führ in meinem Schild'. Špania Dolina, Slovakia, 18th century. Height with lid 14.2 cm. Museum of Decorative Arts, Prague.

the top. They have a round lid often with embossed ornament and handles for easy carrying.

It should also be said that in the eighteenth century, embossed copper plate was also used for monumental sculpture. Some good examples can be found in Germany, especially in Dresden, where there is the equestrian monument of Augustus the Strong of the years 1733—36 made by L. Wiedemann. On the Brandenburg Gate in Berlin stands the Quadriga, made by G. Schadow in the years 1789—94.

In the eighteenth century another piece of interest to collectors appeared, 'španiodolinské poháry' (Špania Dolina beakers), which were made on the territory that is now Slovakia. Copper was smelted in the vicinity of the town of Banská Bystrica by the fifteenth century.

In the sixteenth century some 23 — 29 tons of good quality copper was gained by this simple and inexpensive manner of smelting copper with charcoal in the Slovak mines. The earliest dated beaker made in the valley has survived from 1604. Beakers, boxes, cups, plates and other objects were at the time made as souvenirs and sold in Banská Bystrica, in the spa of Sliač and further afield. This explains that relatively more beakers have survived in the neighbouring countries than in Slovakia proper. These beakers were clearly not made by expert coppersmiths but by the workers in the ore mines. The production and sale of these original souvenirs was their private business, and the mine owners permitted it as it was good publicity for them. In the early nineteenth century the production of these beakers came to an end. The last dated piece is from 1814. The mines, which were in public ownership from 1546, were closed down in 1888 as unprofitable.

From the seventeenth century onwards, objects of sheet brass appeared, which in quality were no less good than those of copper-plate. Sheet brass appeared in the northern and western parts of Europe while the south and east were mainly using copper. As popular as bronze was for decorative objects and household utensils, it was now no longer used for articles of daily use. It continued as the material for the production of cauldrons on three legs, and for mortars even though iron began to

be used in the place of bronze or brass. Brass was used in the production of smoothing irons, which were made by brass specialists in Nuremberg from the second half of the eighteenth century onwards and which were exported in large numbers to the whole of Europe. Most surviving irons are from Nuremberg. This can be deduced from various inscriptions and decorations which usually include the name of the owner of the iron. There were two types of irons, varying according to the source of heat. One group was heated with charcoal. It is easy to distinguish this group as they always have holes in the upper part to enable air to reach the hot embers in the centre of the iron. The second type used heat from a metal, usually iron core which was heated on the stove and placed hot into the smoothing iron. These two types survived long into the nineteenth century and in some parts were still in use in the twentieth century.

Another type of smoothing iron was heated simply by being placed straight on the stove. As to form, the development of these irons was in no ways striking. The earliest surviving pieces were boat-shaped. It is clear that the preceding development of this shape will have been a long one, though, unfortunately, we possess no record of this since the first dated pieces come only from the sixteenth century. The construction of the handle may be a guide as they were made in two ways, either cast in one piece or made from two turned braces holding a wooden handle. M. Viswe drew attention to the various shapes of the handles in the eighteenth century — some had two female figures with an acanthus tendril, other handles were covered with flowers, leaves, little roses or stylized lilies. One form that was particularly popular had two joined figures of dolphins. This style was already known in the early eighteenth century and was still sold by the Nuremberg firm of Ebermeyer in the years 1830—40.

Other objects popular with collectors include snuff boxes. A great deal of research has been devoted to these. The basic work is that of P. Kirnbauer and R. Steiskal-Pauer. These boxes are attractive for their ornamentation and elegant combination of the materials used. The lid and bottom of the box is usually made of sheet brass while the sides are of sheet copper.

111 Brass plate-warmer in the shape of a pan with wooden handles and a double base on three legs. Germany, end of 18th century. Diameter 20 cm. Museum of Decorative Arts, Prague.

These little snuff boxes began to appear in Europe at the end of the seventeenth century when the consumption of tobacco was spreading. The first were made in the Netherlands. Products from there have characteristic engraved ornaments, mostly biblical scenes which corresponded to the dominant Protestant character of local society. Unfortunately none of the boxes bear a mark, and it has not been as yet possible to determine exactly where these boxes were produced. Judging by the quality of the ornamentation it has been suggested that, at first, they were decorated by amateur engravers, i.e. the owners themselves. Later, professional craftsmen took over. M. Wiswe states that typical Dutch products are some 15 cm long, 8 cm wide and about 5 cm high. The most popular shape was oval, but pentagons, octagons and even round ones were made.

After the middle of the eighteenth century production shifted to the town of Iserlohn in northern Rhineland-Westphalia. It is assumed by scholars that the production of snuff boxes was started at Iserlohn to restrict imports from the Netherlands. The products from this town imitated Dutch patterns in their engraved ornament inscriptions. With the introduction of new techniques of decoration, i.e. relief stamping of motifs using a steel embossing die, it became possible to change ornaments and subjects. This made the Iserlohn boxes very popular, and they were exported on a large scale to the neighbouring countries, mainly to Austria and also to Sweden, England and even the Netherlands. A report of the year 1754 shows that the inventor of this manner of ornamentation was Johann Heinrich Giese (1716—61), an embosser and engraver. The production of Iserlohn snuff boxes reached its climax in the middle of the eighteenth century. The producers adapted their motifs to the wishes of the customers who ordered them. For export

135

112 Avignon clock. Cast,
chased and gilded to
a design by sculptor Louis
Simon Boizot by Pierre
Gouthière. Paris, 1771.
Wallace Collection, London.

113 Copper vessel with brass spout and
attachments for iron handle, which used to
be hung above a washbasin. Popular in
Switzerland where it was called
'Brunnenkesselchen'. Switzerland, c. 1700.
Height 28 cm. Museum of the City of
Prague.

137

114 Copper vessel for cooling wine or
other beverages, with hammered decorations.
Between the acanthus there are mascaroons,
the coat-of-arms of the guild of maltsters and
the year 1743. Height 32 cm. Museum of the
City of Prague.

115   Detail of the decoration on the cooler
on photo No. 114.

116 Oval copper container with hammered
sculpture of lions on the lid. Central Europe,
18th century. 15.5×11×10.5 cm. National
Museum, Prague.

117 Copper bottle with a screw top. The
coat-of-arms of the Prague family of
Wunschwitz and the letter 'W' below
a crown on the outside. The pewter top has
the mark of the pewterer and the year 1732.
Prague. Height 29 cm. Museum of the City
of Prague.

141

118 Copper tripod with an iron handle for
use on an open fire. Central Europe, 18th
century. Height excluding the handle
30.5 cm. Private collection, Prague.

142

119   Table heater of copper, with
a wooden handle, which used charcoal.
Central Europe, end of 18th century. Largest
diameter 18.5 cm. Museum of the City of
Prague.

120 A set of two candlesticks and a clock.
The clock-dial has the words 'V^{or}
PAILLARD /F^t DES BRONZES /
PARIS'. The sculpture on the clock is signed
'CLODION / Michel Claude, 1738—1814'.
France, end of 18th century. Sylva-Taroucca
Palace, Prague.

to Austria they depicted events concerning the state of Austria, similarly, scenes from English or Swedish history, were sent to these countries. Apart from J. H. Giese other producers of snuff boxes in Iserlohn were J. H. Hamer, J. A. Keppelmann, J. H. Becker, C. Marmé and J. van Kampen.

In the second half of the eighteenth century, production of similar snuff boxes began in Sweden, following the Iserlohn shape and ornamentation. These Swedish products are often decorated with subjects taken from the calendar or almanachs. The marks on the snuff boxes give the name of the producers: Göran Hedenström, Johan Hedenström and his son Wilhelm, Gabriel Iser and Carl Norman.

The Iserlohn snuff boxes were exported also to Britain. Local producers also began to produce similar boxes, among them Matthew Boulton (1728—1809), whose factory in Birmingham was producing 'bath' metal boxes. They were stamped out by a heat process and, with the use of a substitute alloy, were half the cost of those made of brass.

At the end of the seventeenth and in

121   Jewel-box of gilded brass. The lid and sides of the box are decorated with engraved figures of the personified virtues. On the lid: FIDES (Faith) and IUSTICIA (Justice). On the front: CHARITAS (Charity) and PRUDENTIA (Prudence). On the back: FORTIDVTO (Fortitude) and a figure without an inscription, but, to judge by the attributes it is TEMPERATIA (Temperance). On the right side there is the figure of SPES (Hope) and on the left PACIENCIA (Patience). Austria or southern Germany, last quarter of 19th century. Width 7.2 cm, depth 4.7 cm, height 4.4 cm. Private collection, Prague.

the early eighteenth century other objects began to be made of copper, for example mould and baking tins. These copper examples followed the shape of wooden or pottery forms. Production was made possible by the growth of copper mining when the forges at the end of the sixteenth century began to supply sheet-metal from which the coppersmith could fashion various vessels and cake tins. This brought copper moulds and tins within reach of the ordinary family. A large number of these tins have survived from the nineteenth century, and their shape, size and subject matter show an immense variety. Today it is not possible to say for what occasions these items were used. In addition, no detailed regional study of copper moulds has been carried out, which might provide a clear picture. This is stressed by M. Wiswe, who reached the conclusion that the depiction of biblical themes is rare while folk customs, folklore and religious themes appear more often, e.g. the lamb as symbol of Easter.

Other tins associated with the period of Lent such as fishes and crabs were widespread and were produced over a long period. M. Wiswe is of the opinion that the shape of a fish twisted in a circle was made according to another pattern, perhaps in the graphic arts. It appeared simultaneously in northern Germany, Bohemia and Austria. It is not clear whether the grapevine, another popular shape of copper dishes, can be associated with the Community of the Lord or with Christ in the sense of biblical symbolism. The melon, and particularly the pineapple were popular nineteenth century shapes and are clearly related to the import of goods from the colonies, which few could afford.

Brief mention should be made of a cake tin for a style of cake that is still popular in Bohemia and Austria. It has always been baked in a relatively high tin, circular in shape with fluted sides and a 'funnel' in the centre to ensure it bakes through. This 'funnel' is absent in the oldest pieces and did not appear until the second half of the eighteenth century.

Copper moulds and tins were popular until the First World War and in every good household were kept on the kitchen walls. Lined with a layer of tin, they were highly polished and with their striking copper colour were an attractive feature in the kitchen. They were not easy to make and a later chapter is devoted to the exacting work of the coppersmith.

The Nineteenth and Twentieth Centuries

122 Hanukkah lamp also used on Saturdays. The back is formed of two stags turned towards the middle, the sides are in the shape of lions. Brass. Poland, *c.* 1800. Height 31 cm. State Jewish Museum, Prague.

The nineteenth century was a period of revolutionary change in Europe politically, economically and, by no means least, culturally. In the second half of the century industry underwent a major upswing and began to use new materials for its products. Most of them were cheaper than copper, brass or bronze. These metals and their alloys were mostly limited to the production of art works or luxury decorative objects. In the second half of the century they were used for many exacting and major purposes, and in this chapter we are going to trace the general artistic development that products of copper, brass and bronze followed, but as part of general development.

European art in the nineteenth century was dominated by a style that is today generally called Empire. It is, in fact, the last phase of Neo-Classical art, whose competition with radical Baroque we traced throughout the seventeenth and eighteenth century, and France once again played a decisive role in its crystallization and formation. Empire became the official art of Napoleonic France and was supreme in European art until the late 1820s. The major role in the emergence of the new style must be ascribed to two architects, P. F. L. Fontaine (1762 to 1853) and C. Percier (1764—1838). Together they spent the years 1786—92 in Rome where they studied the monuments of Antiquity. On their return they became the leading architects of the Napoleonic Empire in the years 1794—1814. They published their views on the creation of the Empire style in a joint book *Recueil de décorations intérieures* of 1812.

At that point, Antiquity became a unifying factor in the arts. Ornamental decorations were intentionally and faithfully based on the patterns of ancient monuments, and the shaping of vessels and other objects succumbed to this strong influence. Napoleon's expedition to Egypt roused interest, also, in the cultural sphere. The leading representative of bronze founders and embossers of the French Empire style was P. P. Thomire (1751—1843), who was mentioned in an earlier chapter. Around 1800, his works showed a leaning towards the strict Roman style, as Empire was described at the time. He chiefly made small objects for in-

122 Hanukkah lamp also used on Saturdays. The back is formed of two stags turned towards the middle, the sides are in the shape of lions. Brass. Poland, *c.* 1800. Height 31 cm. State Jewish Museum, Prague.

He worked to designs by leading Empire artists such as P. F. L. Fontaine and Ch. Percier and also made his own. The precision of casting and the perfection of embossing (he was Gouthière's best student) made his workshop famous. He made, to cite examples, a dressing table in 1810, which was intended as the gift of the Paris Town Council for Empress Marie Louise. It was made in collaboration with J. B. C. Odiot to a design by P. P. Prudhon. He also made the bronze ornaments for the 'Marshall Table', dated 1805, made for Napoleon, to which C. Percier supplied the design.

Around 1820 the terse shape of Empire vessels based on a simple cylinder, declined in popularity, and it was supplanted by the Late Empire form. Barrel and semi-barrel shapes made their appearance. The outside of the vessels were no longer smooth and the surface was now divided by relief ribs or convex patches in the shape of drops. Among decorative objects, copies of ancient vessels became popular for vases. All these transformations were applied on objects cast or made of copper or brass. At that time, copper and brass household objects were being rapidly replaced by earthenware and porcelain, which, thanks to the rapid growth of the porcelain industry, were now sold at a price that most people could afford. But even with the narrowing field, copper and brass remained essential and popular materials in the production of certain objects. For example, candlesticks were usually made of brass. The stem was column-shaped, straight, with restrained fluted ornament or with simple decorations following the patterns of Antiquity. There also existed figural stems, where archaic Greek or Egyptian sculpture served as the pattern. The artistic views of the

123 Inkwell in the Louis XVI style. Three glass containers adorned with brass mounts set in a black polished wooden panel on four brass feet. The wooden panel is decorated with six brass mounts in the shape of lyres. All the brass parts are gilded. France, end of 18th century. Length 21.3 cm, width 14 cm, height 13 cm. Museum of Decorative Arts, Prague.

124 Table alarm-clock.
The circular case is of gilded
bronze on four legs in the
shape of paws. Signed
'Johann Müller in Prag'.
C. 1800. Height 14 cm.
Museum of the City of
Prague.

times are reflected also on other objects made of sheet-brass. For instance, table hot-plates, where only the air vents shaped in the form of meanders, palmettes, stylized tendrils etc., reveal the date the object came into existence. Jugs, dishes, sugar bowls and all manner of tableware, if made of copper or brass, deliberately followed the pattern of products of silver or porcelain. Cast bronze and brass held a more exclusive position, often gilded for furniture-making, where these two alloys were used as contrast to the smooth and polished wooden parts. The golden colour of the brass mounts stood out well in the case of black stained furniture and were often of figural or ornamental shape. Here, too, a frequent motif was the eagle's head and figures inspired by Egyptian sculpture. It was characteristic of the time that copper receded into the background and was used largely in the kitchen and work rooms.

Around 1830, a relatively speedy change took place in European art. The balanced, restrained and largely geomet-

125　Two bronze gilt candlesticks with
figures of amorettes climbing a flagstaff.
After Louis Léopold Boilly in the style of the
First Empire. France, early 19th century.
Height 62 cm. Musée Marmottan, Paris.

126 Elm table decorated
with figures of caryatids
made of gilt bronze. The
other decorations are of the
same gilt bronze. The bronze
parts and mounts are the
work of P.-Ph. Thomire.
Signed 'Jacob Desmalter/rue
meslée'.
Paris, before 1813. Height
92 cm, length 140 cm, depth
73 cm. Grand Trianon,
Versailles.

rical shapes of vessels gave way to spa-
cious and heavy forms with restless and
angled outlines. The smooth sides were
now covered with pseudo-Rococo cartouche ornaments, with volutes and rocaille. These new art forms drew shame-
lessly on the Rococo style of the middle of
the eighteenth century and so they were
termed Second Rococo. They again came
from France and rapidly took root in the
whole of Europe.

Works in the Second Rococo style

should not be underestimated. On the
other hand, one cannot overlook the fact
that when it became generally used for
shaping and decorating objects of the applied arts in the middle of the nineteenth
century, factory production took over
these shapes. The result was more than
deplorable. For the first time 'kitsch' in
the modern sense of the word was produced. The Second Rococo style did not
make wide use of copper and brass. Occasionally brass was used for candlesticks

151

and decorative objects, but it rose to the fore only in the second half of the century.

The Second Rococo style is basically one of the results of the period of Romanticism in the arts and crafts. The roots of Romanticism can be traced far back into the eighteenth century where it emerges in literature. From the early nineteenth century it began to pervade all spheres of culture and the arts.

The arts and crafts, and therewith products of bronze, brass and copper, were used widely as decorations for Neo-Gothic interiors, particularly for the production of household goods.

In the meantime, a major international event was being planned, which unexpectedly brought new stimuli to period endeavours. On the first of May 1851 the Great Exhibition of Works of Industry of all Nations was opened in London. The exhibition had been under preparation from 1847 on instigation of H. Cole and his friends. Its aim was to show the potential of modern industry and display examples of good design. All expected to see the results of technical advancement in the sphere of the art but, unfortunately, the Great Exhibition only highlighted the decline of the arts and crafts. This shocking discovery roused a strong response in the whole of Europe but chiefly in Britain, the country holding the exhibition. The only way out of this situation seemed to be to renew the artistic feelings and technical skill of craftsmen and, on the other hand, to show the ordinary public good quality works of craftsmanship of the past as examples of good taste, artistic talent and technical skill. As a consequence, the Victoria and Albert Museum was opened in South Kensington in London in 1852, and it became the first institution to uphold this new idea. After a brief hesitation, other European cities followed suit by setting up similar institutions. The first

127 Smoothing irons from the first half of the 19th century. The iron at the back uses charcoal, the others have a metal core. Central Europe. Museum of the City of Prague.

128 Detail of the smoothing iron in picture No. 127 on the left.

museum of this type on the Continent was established in Vienna in 1863, it was followed in 1867 by Munich and Berlin, in 1874 by Hamburg and then by other cities. These museums of decorative art became one of the stimuli that gave rise to a specific art movement in the second half of the nineteenth century, Historicism. Other influences encouraged the development of the decorative arts, mainly the work of art theoreticians and architects who dealt not only with architecture but regarded the environment as needing a unified approach from the arts.

One of the leading theoreticians of the time was the German architect Gottfried Semper (1803—79). In the 1860s he published the demand that newly created

153

works, based on the pattern of Antiquity, should serve modern Man as well as they served the people of the past. It did not suffice, he believed, to simply copy the decorations and shapes of a given style.

The demands of the theoreticians and the practical steps of enthusiasts brought about an unexpected reaction. The public began to see the artifacts of past ages as perfect products both artistically and in regard to craftsmanship. This enchantment with works of the past gave rise to a broad wave of collecting. Everything was collected that had the mark of an antique. For that reason, one cannot overlook the impact of collecting on art in the second half of the nineteenth century. The circle of collectors increased steadily and could no longer be satisfied with genuine objects of Antiquity. Thus, copies of these

129 Two typical articles of kitchenware from the first half of the 19th century. Copper salt-box to be hung on the wall, adorned with engraving and the date 1815, and brass mortar from roughly the same date. Central Europe. Height of salt-box with back 26 cm. Museum of Decorative Arts, Prague.

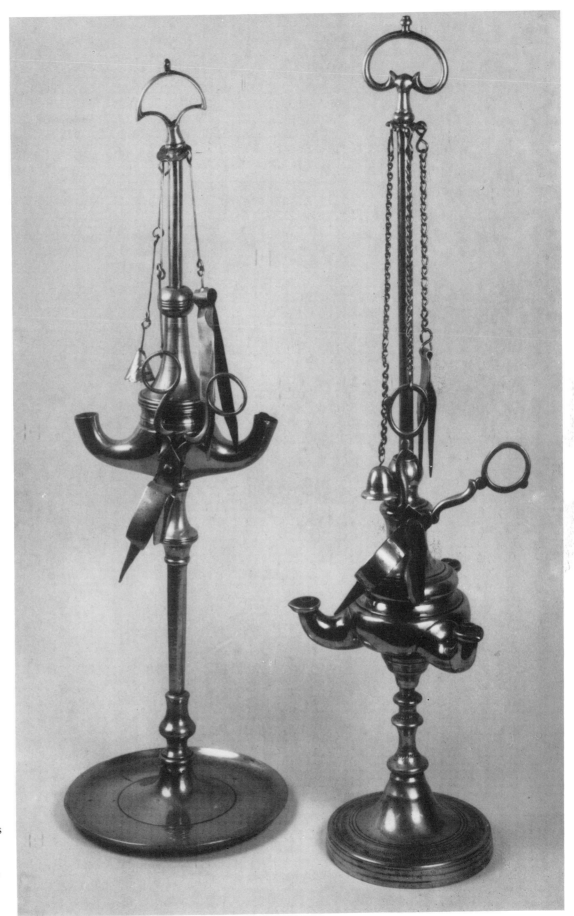

130 Two brass lamps of
the Florentine type with
three oil burners.
A wick-cutter on a chain is
attached to each lamp as
well as damper tweezers.
Southern Europe, c. 1800.
Height 44.5 and 44 cm.
State Jewish Museum,
Prague.

began to be made, often to a high standard of craftsmanship. The production of these copies inevitably led to an increased interest in forgotten techniques, such as enamel, filigree, granulation, mainly on articles for demanding collectors. The market for the general public was still flooded with mechanically imitated substitutes. This period is important for today's collector since it was then that forgeries began to appear in large numbers to deceive the inexperienced collector.

The success of the Great Exhibition in London aroused a great response in the world, and within a short period similar exhibitions were held in other European countries. France organized a world exhibition in Paris in 1855, a second one was opened in London in 1862, in Dublin in 1865, in Vienna in 1873 and so on. From 1904 until the First World War such exhibitions were held almost every year. It was typical of the atmosphere of the time that these big exhibitions tried to encom-

131 Brass Empire candlestick with a square base decorated with astragal ornaments. Bohemia, *c.* 1820. Height 21 cm. Museum of the City of Prague.

132 Round lamp of sheet
brass with an oil burner.
Germany (?), *c.* mid 19th
century. Height 11.5 cm.
Museum of the City of
Prague.

pass the broadest sphere of human activity and arts and crafts played a major role. The cultural level of the exhibiting country was judged by the quality of objects of the decorative arts on exhibition.

The comparison of artistic endeavours and the creative tendencies in various parts of the world inevitably influenced the further development of the arts and crafts. The world exhibitions played the role of mediator. As a consequence, the

craftsmanship of the time is sometimes called the work of the 'epoch of the world exhibitions'.

To return to the middle of the nineteenth century, European arts and crafts were still under the influence of the Second Rococo style, and this was fostered primarily by the porcelain works of Central Europe. France still remained the leading force. During the reign of Emperor Napoleon III, in the early 1860s, the

158

134 Detail of the
Hanukkah lamp in picture
No. 133.

134 Detail of the Hanukkah lamp in picture No. 133.

133 Hanukkah lamp which also served as a Saturday candlestick. The back part is an architectural form from Eastern Europe. Poland (?), first half of 19th century. State Jewish Museum, Prague.

Second Rococo style began to be rejected, having become an example of undisciplined and artistically unbalanced work. The Renaissance then became a binding pattern and architects, as well as decorators, were to use it as a model. At first it was not imitated literally, the decorators and ornamentalists used Renaissance decorative features merely as inspiration, but, after the mid-sixties, the example of the Renaissance became so powerful that works were produced as exact copies.

In the 1870s French domination of the arts was, for a time, interrupted. The defeat of France in the Franco-Prussian War was not only a military failure but France fell back from its leading position in European culture. Viennna became the new centre of art, deriving advantage from its position as the capital of the vast multinational monarchy. The Director of the Vienna Kunsthistorisches Museum, Rudolf von Eitelberger, gathered around him a group of artists and architects who regarded the early Italian Renaissance as the ideal pattern and starting point for new works of art. Thanks to broad and well organized art schooling throughout the monarchy, the views of this leading group penetrated to even remote corners of the Empire. At the world exhibition in Vienna in 1873, Austria presented a unified style in all spheres of the arts and crafts, and in mass production, major success was reaped in the production of glass, in goldsmiths' work, the production of furniture and also in decorative work in bronze. This unity of art work from many professions brought a great response in Europe, and contemporaries thought it worth copying. It should be said, however, that the Austrian attempt to introduce a unified style for all branches of the arts and crafts did not lead to ultimate success. Formal restrictions limited creative freedom and did not stimulate further

135 Typical brass candlesticks from the late 19th century. The popularity of candlesticks of this shape lasted into the early 20th century. Central Europe. Height 20 and 21 cm. Museum of the City of Prague.

160

136 Bronze inkwell.
Gilded and black painted.
France, first half of 19th
century. Height 19.5 cm.
Private collection, Prague.

137 Two Empire brass
candlesticks with stems in
the shape of caryatids.
Austria (?), first quarter of
19th century. Height 21 cm.
Museum of the City of
Prague.

138 Two sugar-bowls of sheet brass.
Central Europe, before mid 19th century.
Height of the larger bowl 8.5 cm. Museum of
the City of Prague.

139   Two typical jugs of the early 19th
century. Copper plate. Central Europe.
Height of the larger jug 39 cm. Museum of
the City of Prague.

140 Empire bronze
candlestick combined with
a glass sculpture of
a dolphin. Bohemia (?),
c. 1820. Height 26.5 cm.
Museum of Decorative Arts,
Prague.

141   Set of baking tins for cakes and
puddings. Central Europe, 19th century.
Diameter of the cake tin 26.5 cm. Museum
of the City of Prague.

142   Brass writing set. Gilded and black
patinated. Made by the Prague craftsman
Isák. Prague, early 19th century. Museum of
the City of Prague.

143 Altar candlestick in the Neo-Renaissance style. Designed by B. Wachsman, 1863. Height 42 cm. Church of SS Cyril and Methodius, Prague.

144 Hammered water
container in copper plate.
Brass tap. Moravia, *c.* 1880.
Height 26.5 cm. State Jewish
Museum, Prague.

experiments. The Neo-Renaissance was
not the basis of further development but,
in its way, a culmination which did not
lead to continued creative achievements.
Furthermore, according to the ideas of the
period, each style was to serve a specific
task. Serious theoretical studies were published suggesting specific historical styles
for the furnishing of dining rooms, par-
lours and bedrooms. The Romanesque or
Gothic style was regarded as fitting for ecclesiastical buildings and their furnishings.
It is clear that the arts and crafts faced
major tasks. Entire buildings of pseudo-
historical churches and cathedrals were
furnished in a unified style following the
spirit of the building itself. The result was
large numbers of Romanesque candlesticks, candelabras, eternal lights, incense
burners, incense holders, baptismal fonts
and other furnishings, often designed by
leading artists. Bronze, brass and copper

were widely used for this purpose. Similar requirements were put forward for the newly built secular residences and salons. Copper, brass and bronze was used to make vases, jardinières, dishes, candlesticks, decorative plates, gargoyles, fountains and other decorative objects, more or less faithful copies of the Baroque, Renaissance and other styles.

Bronze and brass also found wide application in the technical sphere. The introduction of gas for lighting stimulated the production of chandeliers and lamps made of these alloys since they suited the technical requirements of gas pipes. Hammered brass or copper plate was suitable as the cover for electricity lighting equip-

ment. Such lamps and chandeliers were made to perfection in small workshops and factories in Vienna, Munich, Berlin and Paris.

The second half of the nineteenth century did not see exclusively historical styles. When the Anglo-French forces conquered Peking in 1860 and the victorious armies looted the treasures of the Summer Palace and brought them to Europe, Chinese art roused a great response among European artists. The same is true of Japanese art, which was presented to the Europeans at the world exhibitions. From 1862 antique Japanese art could be seen at almost every world exhibition. Japanese art was appreciated in Europe,

145 Copper candlestick with an adjustable holder for the candle known as a 'patent' holder in use by the 18th century. Central Europe, c. mid 19th century. Height 18.5 cm. Museum of the City of Prague.

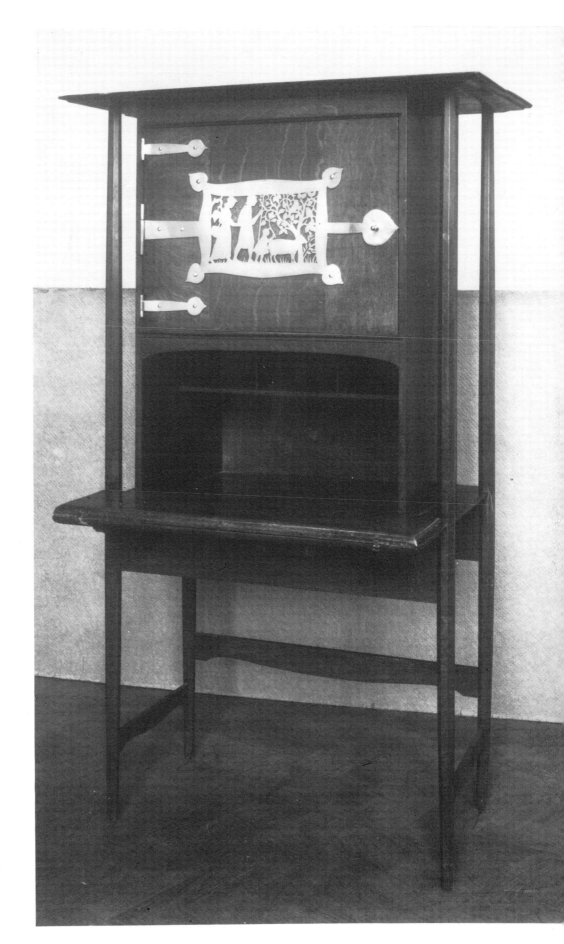

146 Writing desk of
unpolished and unstained
oak, decorated with copper
mounts. To a design by
C. F. A. Voysey. England,
1896. Victoria and Albert
Museum, London.

particularly the close link between Japanese art and nature.

The end of the 1870s and 1880s were not influenced only by Japanese art. European traditions remained very strong. Some European artists turned again to Baroque and Rococo, as they assumed that these historical styles would give as much opportunity for improvisation and creative fantasy as the Far Eastern approach to the arts. In many spheres of culture this return was welcomed, not because they lacked the courage to move along new paths but because emotional ties and historical conditions linked them closely to the past. This explains the success of Neo-Baroque and the Third Rococo style, as this return to the past is sometimes called, particularly in the countries of Central Europe.

This way proved artistically a dead end as had the Viennese attempt at the Neo-Renaissance in the 1870s. At the end of that century the Arts and Crafts movement had at their disposal an elaborate and theoretically organised system of all European styles, but these historicizing trends had, by that time, exhausted their creative and inspiring strength. The constant application of well-tested types and shapes led to general fatigue and consequent stereotypes.

Shortly before 1900 it became clear that new impulses were coming from Britain where new ways were being sought and success reaped in efforts at reform.

147   Art Nouveau copper vessel with two handles. Germany (?), c. 1900. Height 25 cm. Museum of Decorative Arts, Prague.

148 Art Nouveau copper 'samovar'. Austria, *c.* 1903. Height 33.5 cm. Museum of Decorative Arts, Prague.

Two people introduced these new ideas: John Ruskin and William Morris, who, from the 1860s, were the leading personalities in British arts and crafts. The first success was in the 1880s, when book layouts by A. H. Mackmurdo roused attention. In the 1890s the core of these reform efforts shifted to Glasgow where the centre of a new style formed in the Group of Four centered round Charles R. Mackintosh. These new ideas put forward by the Group of Four were spread through journals and exhibitions. This was one of the reasons why the new style quickly spread from Scotland to Belgium, then to Germany, France and other countries of Europe so that by 1900 it had covered Europe as a whole. It assumed different names in individual countries and became known as 'Jugendstil' in Germany, 'Sezessionstil' in Austria, in France as 'Art Nouveau', while it was called 'Modern Style'

173

in Britain and Russia. The aesthetics of the new style turned against the historical approach. The Modern Style was an effort to shape the modern environment as it related to the mentality of Man at the end of the nineteenth century. Without anyone realizing it, it became the last unified style of art in Europe. It affected all spheres of the arts, ranging from architecture to sculpture and painting and the applied arts. In the arts and crafts, i.e. in products of bronze, brass and copper, the traditional form was cast away. The new style quite uncompromisingly affected decorations, removing the historical schemes and re-placing it with a new conception of ornamentation, mostly influenced by stylized plant features. Nature alone was regarded as the source of the artist's inspiration, and the shape of an object was relaxed to its function. Today, with the passing of time, we know that Art Nouveau ornamentation drew heavily on Japanse coloured woodcuts, so popular in Europe from the 1870s and the decoration on Islamic ceramics. A few stimuli came from the stylization used in Minoan art, which was discovered at that time. The strong role played by tradition is shown on Late Gothic European woodcuts, whose plant ornaments influenced the artists who followed the new style. Even if scholars have traced the sources of inspiration of Art Nouveau, the fact remains that the historical style was overcome by around 1900. Objects of bronze, brass and copper and those of other materials were used merely as parts of interior decorations and in conception underlined the unity of style. Designs of even the smallest interior decorations were often the work of leading representatives of the movement. But the new style faced the same danger as earlier ones, namely that it could become simply a short lived fashion as soon as it was adapted by factories and small workshops. The leading artists soon realized this danger and decided to face it in the British style. As early as 1897 a 'Vereinigte Werkstätten für Kunst und Handwerk' (Joint Arts and Crafts Workshop) was set up in Munich, whose founders took inspiration from the ideas of William Morris. In 1902 the Grand-Duke of Weimar summoned Henri van de Velde who set up an Arts and Crafts Seminar (Kunstgewerbliches Seminar), a teaching centre out of which, after 1918, grew the famous Bauhaus. In 1903, a Wiener Werkstätte (Vienna Workshop) was established in Vienna with the aim of producing individual works of art, designing entire interiors as well as building houses. Finally, in 1907, an association came into existence in Munich called 'Der Deutsche Werkbund' (German Works Association), which aimed to give publicity in word and deed to raising the standard of products. This association placed stress on unity of form, material and purpose and really belonged already to the next period.

In European art, Art Nouveau came to

149 Two stems of electric lamps of sheet brass. Bohemia, after 1900. Height 28 cm. State Jewish Museum, Prague.

150 Hanukkah candlestick of brass adorned with the relief figure of a lion. Prague, early 20th century. (Clearly inspired by an older pattern.) Height 14 cm. State Jewish Museum, Prague.

a very dramatic end with the First World War, even though the first signs of its decline appeared before 1914. Around 1910 a movement of artists arose in the advanced industrial countries with the main idea of overcoming the contradictions between art and mass production. They were to set examples and provide prerequisites for industry to produce articles that were on a truly artistic level. Naturally, such efforts varied from centre to centre and so did views as to the shape of the object and ornamental and decorative systems. For France, the leader of these ideas, lightness and elegance of ornament became typical, drawing on stimuli from highly varied and often remote sources. Individual elements can be distinguished from Rococo, and also Cubism or Oriental and primitive cultures. On the other hand, Austria, chiefly Vienna, gave preference to décor based on geometrical or plant elements composed in balanced units and set out in a symmetrical manner. Beside these two main centres others existed in Germany, Poland, Sweden and Bohemia, chiefly Prague.

The Prague movement was based on the Artěl co-operative. After 1910 they devised an original style, applying principles of Cubism in painting to all art forms, ranging from house fronts and small objects to architectonic features such as grilles, bannisters and light fittings. Highly remarkable results were achieved in furniture making. This style had no parallel in European art. It was introduced to the European public at an exhibition of the Munich Werkbund held in Cologne in 1914, but as this was the year the First World War broke out, the effects of this Cologne exhibition were to be lost.

Even before the outbreak of the war, serious thought had been given to holding an international exhibition. Paris was interested in organising it, wishing to show the results of these efforts of revival. The outbreak of the war meant the holding of such an exhibition was postponed. It was only in 1925 that an exhibition was inaugurated in Paris under the title Exposition Internationale des Arts Décoratifs et Industriels, in which all countries of Europe participated including the Soviet Union. Only Germany refused to take part. The exhibition was the culmination of the revival movement, the roots of which went back far into the nineteenth century.

Trends in the arts began to show the understanding for factory mass production. They emerged shortly after 1925 and became known as Constructivism and Functionalism. These are, however, matters that concern contemporary applied arts.

A full understanding of the common denominator of the individual styles presented at the Paris exhibition was reached by art historians only on the occasion of an exhibition 'Les Années 1925' held by the Musée des Arts Décoratifs in Paris. It was Y. Brunhammer, who, in writing the catalogue for the exhibition, was the first to use the term 'Art Déco', which was then generally adopted for the style of the twenties.

In these disputes bronze, brass and copper did not play a specific role. They tended to be used more in the production of complementary luxury objects or in costly buildings as material for grilles, bannisters, light fittings and the like, which in their artistic form followed the trends of individual cultural centres. Thus we have become witnesses to bronze, brass and copper playing a far greater role in the present day in technology rather than in the arts.

151 Brass emblem decorating the guild treasury of the Brno brassmakers, showing the tools of their trade and the inscription 'Johann Schneider'. Early 19th century. Height 12.5 cm. Museum of the City of Brno.

Technical Background

This section sets out to look at objects from behind the scenes. The resulting artifacts should not be regarded merely as the work of an unknown metal-founder, metal-embosser or coppersmith but as an achievement in a sphere of human endeavour and art. It is, therefore, important to learn some basic facts about the technical problems involved.

Before we turn to a more detailed description of the work of these craftsmen it might be useful, for the sake of clarity, to deal in brief outline with the history of various techniques.

Generally, it is easier to understand a work made by the hands of Man if one knows how they were made or, if one can be present when they are being produced, but this direct contact with the birth of an artifact is seldom possible for most collectors. Thus, this chapter aims to offer a brief introduction to technical knowledge. However, we know little of how past founders or embossers worked, and many problems will have to be clarified. In the first place, it will be necessary to reconstruct the entire technical process since technology is an integral part of every creative process.

Metal, particularly bronze-casting into a mould, was already known in Egypt at the time of the Middle Kingdom (1991 to 1786 B.C.), as proved by finds of earthenware moulds. The Egyptians knew two techniques of casting. Solid casts, a technology that was suitable only for small objects, and also cire perdue or lost wax, which made far larger casts possible. The Egyptian founders also knew how to bring together large bronze objects after they had been cast in sections or parts.

Small bronze artifacts adorned with incrustation have survived from a later period in Egypt. These objects were inlaid with copper, enamel, gold, silver and an alloy of gold and silver. It is thought that this technique of decoration is of Mesopotamian origin. Far fewer works of hammered metal have survived from ancient Egypt.

Attention should be drawn to a quite unique work, the lifesize portrait statue of Pharaoh Phiopse I and his son Menthesuptis from the period of the Old Kingdom (Sixth Dynasty, before 2263 B.C.). This statue was made on a wooden core and rivets were used to attach the hammered copper plates, each about one to five millimetres in thickness. Some scholars have expressed the opinion that certain of the copper parts were made by casting and not hammering. The hair on the statue was of lapis lazuli, and black and white stones were inserted for the eyes.

The second centre of civilization — Mesopotamia — clearly had a much older tradition in working metals, both metal hammering and founding. The history of metal hammering, in that region, dates from the fourth millennium B.C. and is related to the arrival of the Sumerians, whose empire had a highly advanced civilization. The Sumerians brought the knowledge of working metal from their original home near the Caucasus and the Urals. The Mesopotamian artisans knew how to make both solid and hollow casts, and they used bronze alloys about one thousand years earlier than the Egyptians. By the third millennium B.C. they already knew how to cast copper by the 'cire perdue' method. What is of special importance is that the Mesopotamian bronze-founders treated the raw castings and finished them off by chasing. The ancient Greeks were the direct heirs of such surface treatment of a cast object. In Mesopotamia, too, bronze articles were decorated with incrustation, and among the

152 Liturgical vessel for incense made of sheet brass. In the shape of a boat with legs in the shape of dolphins. Example of Baroque toreutics. Bohemia, 18th century. Height 15.5 cm. Museum of the City of Prague.

various materials used were enamel and precious stones. Naturally, they also knew another technique of ornamentation — engraving. The Mesopotamian technology for casting metal and the art of metal founding laid the foundations for Greek bronze casting. These skills were handed on to Rome and Byzantium and ultimately to medieval Europe.

At the very beginnings the Greeks produced only small bronze castings. Large bronzes are a Greek technical invention that appeared in the sixth century B.C. The technology of metal-casting in ancient Greece reached such sophistication that Europe managed to catch up with it only with objects made in eighteenth-century France. At the beginning, the metal-founders of archaic Greece adopted the east-ern technology of casting, i.e. casting small solid casts or making large ones by the cire perdue technique. This method makes it difficult to heat the mould and melt the wax in the case of large objects. The Greeks solved this problem by abandoning the cire perdue method and inventing a new one called hollow cast, where the main technical novelty, as we shall see below, was a wooden core that could be dismantled. Another important Greek invention was the hard soldering of bronze where the use of rivets to join the individual pieces was no longer needed. The Greek metal-founders had at their disposal a technology that enabled them to cast objects of a size hitherto unknown, and this became most evident in Greek sculpture.

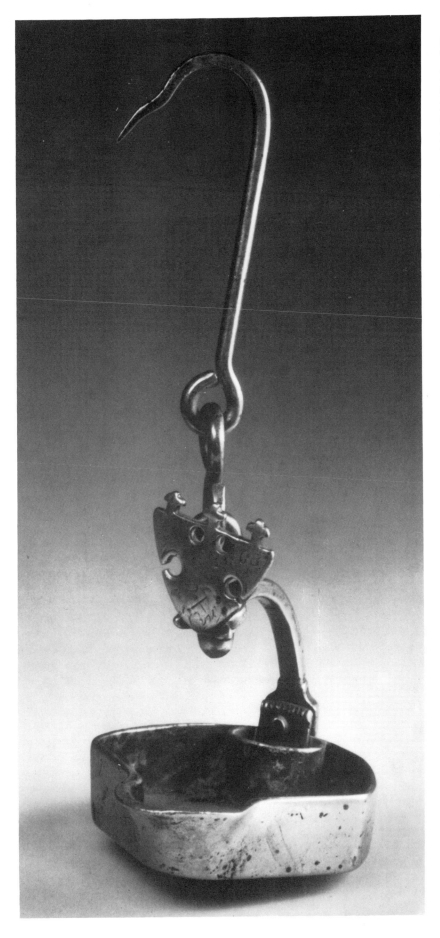

Ancient Rome did not contribute much that was new to founding and metalwork. The products show that the Romans applied both Greek experience and also the advanced skill of the Etruscans. Roman production varies greatly in technical quality and artistic achievement. For the purpose of illustration it should be said that some Roman foundries produced human figures in various postures, without heads, to keep in store. Portrait heads were added on the basis of a definite order so that sometimes a head would fit the body rather incongruously. This confirms that in ancient Rome the art of metal-casting did not advance in technical terms.

The period of the migration of nations brought ruin to Europe especially in the arts. Metal-work continued undisturbed only in Byzantium and the former Roman provinces in the East under its rule. From there technical skills and experiences spread to the countries north of the Alps. It is likely that Bishop Bernwards' foundry in Hildesheim applied a technical tradition that had survived in Byzantium, and Brother Theophilus drew on the same eastern sources. Founders at the court of Charlemagne availed themselves of the technical skill of Antiquity.

It would be a mistake to imagine that the 'barbarian' nations who became bearers of this new art had no technical traditions in working bronze of their own, but they had little in common with Antiquity. We must go back to the Early Bronze Age to find the beginnings of this particular tradition. At that time, a centre of bronze production grew up in the Danube valley, on territory that is now Hungary. The products made there must have been very popular because finds of articles made in the Danube region can be traced in a broad strip across Central Europe and as far as southern Scandinavia. Bronze was hammered and most of the utensils

153 Brass miner's lamp. The monogram I T S is engraved on the handle with two crossed miners' hammers and the year 1763. Example of minor metal-casting work. Bohemia. Height of holder excluding handle 3.5 cm. Museum of Decorative Arts, Prague.

were made in one piece. Larger objects such as buckets and amphoras were assembled from several pieces and riveted together. Similarly, handles were attached with the aid of rivets. The articles produced range from bowls and plates to cauldrons, amphoras, skimmers and ladles. Characteristic ornamental motifs of this work are tiny repoussé ornaments hammered from inside the vessel.

In the Hallstatt period the centre of production of hammered bronze vessels shifted to the south-eastern Alpine region, where figural motifs were added to purely ornamental designs. At that time, home production was supplanted by imports from northern Italy and the Etruscan foundries (situlas, jugs with spouts), which later were imitated in Celtic workshops. When the Germanic tribes drove the Celts out, Roman bronze vessels became widespread in Central, Western and Northern Europe. In the confusion caused by the migration of nations such imports from Italy ceased, and the people in the north of Europe had to search for ways of making their own products. They made use of the technical traditions of Antiquity as interpreted by Byzantium. Bronzes surviving in Germany and the Netherlands show that in technical respects they did not begin anew in the early Middle Ages. The lost wax method of casting was known, but they used solid casts on a much larger scale. As in Antiquity human and animal figures had eyes inlaid with enamel.

In the Gothic period large-sized works such as fountains, tombstones, entire tombs as well as bells were produced. And by their side also small ware, mainly objects used in divine service and household utensils. It is thought that the brazier's models were made of clay, but in the archives there are also records of such models in wood, and surviving pieces have been found. Guild rules laid down that the preparation of such models was the work of the wood-carvers, and the conditions included in the contract insisted on the return of the wooden model, which, after cleaning and possibly replacement of polychrome, could be turned into a work of art. But there are also records showing that the lost wax process was used at the time.

In Renaissance Italy bronze was a very popular material. Until the fifteenth century the technical knowledge of casting, especially of monumental works, was based on experiences of bronze-founders from Byzantium. Yet failures did occur. For that reason the major contribution of the Renaissance in the sphere of metal-casting technology was the invention of a partial mould that could be disassembled and which, in technical terms, perfected the cire perdue process. One model could be used over and over again even when the cast proved a failure. With the inquiring spirit of the Renaissance they managed to overcome many problems in casting large objects, mainly statues, which began to be cast in one piece. Many problems needed to be solved: to find a suitable ceramic material for the mould, the casing and core; a functioning large kiln for heating such a big mould and another one suitable for smelting a large quantity of alloy. The local artisans knew how to patinate and chase bronze. Late Renaissance casts were so perfect that they barely needed tooling.

In the Baroque period the Italian tradition of founding was adopted by France which, in its Neo-Classical concept, moved away from Italian and Central European radical Baroque. French Neo-Classicism made wide use of bronze. The cire perdue process was further perfected and new alloys were put to the test. State art studios were set up in which high technical perfection was achieved and maintained for sculpture as for the arts and crafts. This gave rise to the high quality of French metal-founding in the nineteenth and twentieth century.

In the nineteenth century an important change took place in casting sculptures, later decorative objects and those of daily use. The sculptor supplied a model and the metal-caster saw to the rest, including the patination. The creative work ended with the modelling of the statue or object in clay or plaster of Paris. The specialist metal-founder then reproduced the model supplied as close in likeness and as perfect as possible technically. The sculptor or designer became a fine artist, who devoted himself exclusively to preparatory work before casting, i.e. the creation of a work of art in the form of a model, leaving the actual execution of the work to a technical specialist. This division of work into two entirely separate parts took place in the nineteenth century and sig-

154 Bronze vessel on three legs with
a handle to be hung over the fire. Relief
decorations with the monogram of Christ
and the Virgin Mary and the year 1750.
Example of more exacting metal-casting.
Austria or southern Germany. Height
excluding handle 34 cm. Museum of
Decorative Arts, Prague.

156 Brass candlestick in Neo-Gothic style. Central Europe, after mid 19th century. Height 61.8 cm. Museum of Decorative Arts, Prague.

◁
155 Jacques Caffieri: Design for the ornamentation of the baldaquin or pall of the Paris guild of braziers. Ink drawing on paper. Signed 'Inventé et dessiné par Jacques Caffieri 1715'. 67×49 cm. Musée de Tessé, Le Mans.

157   Art Nouveau copper wine cooler. Jan
Eisenloeffel (?), Netherlands (?), after 1900.
Height 22.5 cm. Museum of Decorative
Arts, Prague.

158 Copper teapot decorated with niello
and brass mounts. Austria (?), *c.* 1900.
Height 22.5 cm. Museum of Decorative Arts,
Prague.

159   Box of hammered brass sheet.
Stamped in the base:
'WIENER/WERK/STATTE' and the
signature of the craftsman Josef Holi.
Vienna, *c.* 1920. Height 12 cm. Museum of
Decorative Arts, Prague.

160   Two boxes of zinc and copper plate.
Signed 'ARTÉL PRAHA'. Designed by
V. Hofman. Prague, 1918. Height 10.5 cm.
Museum of Decorative Arts, Prague.

161 Table lamp of sheet
brass. Designed by J. Gočár.
Prague, first quarter of 20th
century. Height 28.5 cm.
Museum of Decorative Arts,
Prague.

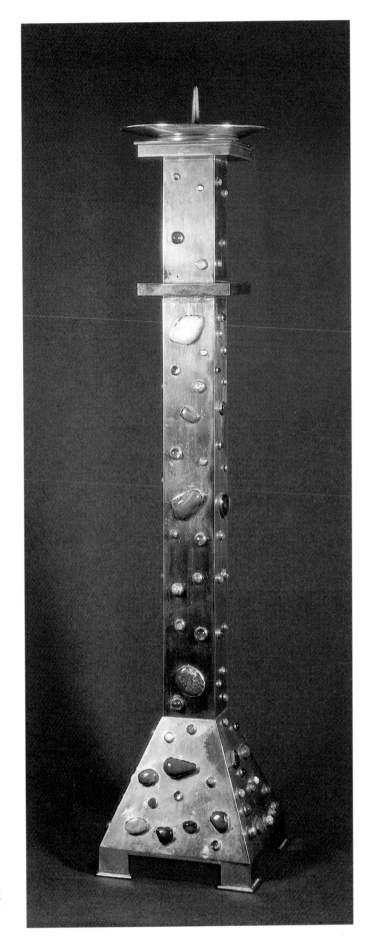

162 Altar candlestick of
brass adorned with polished
semi-precious stones.
Designed by J. Plečnik.
Prague, 1932. Height 48 cm.
Church of the Holy Heart of
the Lord, Prague.

191

164 Seal of the Brno guild of brass-makers. The frieze along the edge holds the inscription 'SIG DER EHRBA KUNST UN HAND DER GELBGISS ZU BRINN 1779'. Diameter 4 cm. Archives of the City of Brno.

163 Example of the chloride corrosion on a bronze object. The metal core of the mortar is almost completely broken down by corrosion. This mortar was excavated in Prague in 1912 close to a spot where saltpetre was produced in the past. Height of the torso 18.5 cm.

naled the new social status of the artist. Metal-casting and hammering became largely acts of reproduction.

From a technical point of view France maintained its leading position. In the eighteenth century the French invented the sand mould, used to this day, which enabled the founder to finally abandon the ancient cire perdue process of casting, which was far more laborious and involved greater cost. The sand mould meant the cast could be split into several parts and the same mould used to make a number of casts, which was not possible by the lost wax process without modelling a new cast in wax. But it should be remembered that the sand mould did not give as faithful a cast as the wax, and the numerous seams of the multipart mould had to be laboriously removed by tooling and polishing. The casting of more intricate shapes in one piece was also more difficult. For that reason some founders returned to the cire perdue process, which became cheaper at the end of the nineteenth century by the insertion of gelatine into the mould.

Metal chisellers, working mostly in copper, dealt with monumental commissions in the nineteenth century. Not that this technology was more advantageous for a given task but because it was relatively cheaper than bronze casting. For, in the case of large objects the costs of casts were high. And, in addition, the artist and metal chiseller were not one and the same person as in the seventeenth and eighteenth centuries; the chiselling, both of monumental statues and objects, was the job of artisans or state workshops examples of which existed in Berlin from the end of the eighteenth century on. Inevitably, the technique of chiselling such monumental works had to be changed. The chiseller did not use a hammer and mallet to chisel the shape into thin metal plate underpinned by a wooden or metal model as had been done for years; he did so with the aid of various measurements, chiselling the smaller parts according to a free-standing model. The parts were then mounted on to a supporting framework.

In conclusion, mention should be made of the galvanoplastic technology, which roused great attention when first introduced. This is basically an electrolytic process, with the aid of which the copper, dissolved in a bath, settled on the inner side of a plaster cast covered with layer of electrically conductive graphite. After a certain time the layer of copper becomes so thick that the plaster mould can be removed. The copper positive corresponds exactly to the negative plaster mould. When the galvanoplastic process was first applied in practice in Petrograd, in the middle of the nineteenth century, it was thought that finally a suitable method had been invented for gaining exact and cheap casts. But it was soon shown that the quality of the copper, which in this process could not be compacted by forging, did not make it possible to expose such an object to the weather or to water. The technical potential, however, led to further experiments when objects of zinc were covered in copper by an electrolytic method, or even gilded or silvered. The cheap zinc was to replace the copper or the even more expensive bronze. Even these experiments were soon abandoned, and the artists returned to bronze and copper with their ability to stress the artistic quality of a work, and all imitations were cast aside. This outline of the history of casting and hammering techniques, the two basic methods of treating metals, makes it clear that toreutics remained, on the whole, unchanged in its technology over the centuries, while casting very soon developed several basic methods.

Technically, the simplest and clearly the oldest method is solid casting.

A mould was made of resistant material, e.g. clay or slate. This mould was made of the plates, and half the future cast was carved in each. By fitting the two panels exactly to each other a hollow resulted into which the melted alloy was poured. This manner of casting had several disadvantages. In the first place, this method used a large amount of valuable material which made objects unnecessarily heavy, and in the case of large casts there was the added danger that damage might be caused by flaws that could arise as the cooling metal contracted. On the other hand, it was possible to make a large number of casts from such a permanent mould, and there was no need to make a new mould for each new cast.

The disadvantage of such casts was overcome by the hollow cast, which is said to have been invented in Antiquity by the sculptors Rhoikos and Theodoros of Samos. There is little doubt that this hollow cast was an invention of the Greeks, who were thus able to cast bronze objects and statues of large size. The Greeks divided the mould into two parts, the casing and the core. They carved the object or statue in wood, which became the actual model and from this they modelled the casing of the mould. To attain a hollow into which the melted metal could be poured they made the original wooden model smaller by scraping or trimming the surface. The core that thus came into being was fixed with iron rods to the casing to keep it firmly in place when the metal was poured in. The wooden core itself had to be divided into two parts so that the individual parts could be taken out of the mould once the metal had cooled. Parts of an object, into which no core could be placed or removed after casting (e.g. the limbs of a statue) were cast separately and were then attached to the statue or object by riveting or brazing.

A very popular process was the cire perdue, or lost wax method of casting because it made it possible to depict even fine details of the model and, once it was perfected, even to cast large objects and statues. For this method of casting a core was made of clay or rough sand and in the case of large object a supporting construction was built, usually of iron wire. On this core all details of the actual objects to be cast were modelled. The thickness of the layer of wax, mostly 3—5 mm, corresponded to that of the wall of the future cast. In fact, the wax model was the original one, and it was modelled and covered with a layer of fine clay and then further layers of clay, for the composition of which there existed many a formula. The founder had to pay attention to the wax and vent pipes which he modelled with the aid of wax threads and string of the required size. A mould thus made was left to dry and then was heated in a kiln. The hot wax ran out of the mould and left a hollow, which the founder could now fill with the liquid metal. Such a cast could be taken out of the mould only after the latter had been cut to pieces. The heating of the wax model and the destruction of the model led to this technology becoming known as the cire perdue, that is lost wax casting process.

Over the centuries special modelling techniques were worked out such as a copying technique of casting, which the Romans devised for copying Greek originals. This technology involved a plaster negative form being taken from the original, its inside covered with a layer of wax and on it rough-grained sand was strewn to form a core proper. After the removal of the plaster negative, the sand core remained covered with a negative mould in wax, and now the founder could continue work as for the cire perdue process.

Another known method was casting into a bed of sand; this was used for flat casts such as doors and tiles and the molten metal was poured into a bounded, flat open mould, into the bottom of which ornamental relief motifs has been impressed.

In the Foundry

The first and basic task a metal-founder had to perform on receiving an order was to make a mould. The choice of material for such a mould was determined by the size of the object to be cast and the experience of the founder himself. Sand was used for small objects, clay for larger objects. Throughout the Middle Ages, clay was the basic material for moulds. This was made from a mixture of loam and fine quartz sand. This moulding material had to satisfy high demands and in most areas, it was very difficult to find such sand with ideal qualities for casting. Often it could not be attained at all as it needed to be non-greasy, but not sterile, not too hard or too soft and yet without pebbles; it needed to be easily shaped and keep its compactness when fired. As a result, the founder had to use available material to make a mixture that fitted his needs. There existed all manner of formulas for the preparation of a suitable mixture. They varied at different times and according to local conditions as well as the experiences of given workshops. The Italian metal-founder Biringuccio (1480—1538) recommended that up to two thirds of cloth shearings be added to the moulding clay. The Bohemian Master Křička (†1570) used horse hair and dropping to form the core of the clay, finishing it with the hair and dung of cattle. Others preferred waste from wool carding or coarse hair from fulling cloth. Formulas even include crushed bricks, rust or ground forge scale, ash from a ram's horn or potash. And this list is by no means conclusive.

The process was similar in making sand moulds. The founder here, too, gave preference to a mixture of various kinds of sand, again with the addition of different materials that would give the mixture the required quality. Biringuccio recommended the mixture of one third ash of ram's horn, added to carefully washed sand baked in the kiln, and, in addition one twelfth of old well-sifted flour. Everything was thoroughly mixed and moistened with urea or wine. A frame or wooden box was then filled with this matter, and the required mould shaped from it, and then dried.

Once the mould has been made, its surface was painted so that the individual parts of the mould might later be easily disassembled and taken to pieces. Křička recommends various formulas, which all have vine-ash as a base, with various other additives such as salt and vinegar or wine vinegar, chalk, ash and the ash of a burnt calves head, or milk and white of egg, etc. Often a coat of melted suet was applied.

Once he had made the mould, the founder turned to the actual casting of the object. We already know that the artisan of old knew many types of alloys. He therefore had to select the one that, in quality, best fitted the object in hand. Knowledge of the qualities of these alloys was an essential prerequisite of the founder, and it was up to him to decide which alloy to use in making a certain object. This knowledge was naturally one of the secrets of the founder's craft, and only general data can be culled from written instructions. This was well expressed by

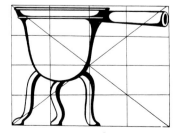

The casting of every-day articles was carefully prepared as to construction. Based on a drawing in an instructional handbook from the 1560s.

165 Shop sign of brazier G. Carlson. Oil on metal. Sweden, *c.* 1800. 73×63 cm. Nordiska Museet, Stockholm.

Tools used for the smelt: rod with a clay plug, tapping bar, slag skimmer, chuck collet, shovel and tongs. Based on a drawing in a manuscript from the 1560s.

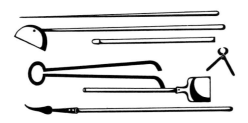

Biringuccio: 'Think first for what purpose you need the alloy and then stipulate the ratio so as to correspond to your conviction and experience.' Before initiating the actual casting, several other tasks had to be attended to. First, the quantity of material needed, secondly, its quality. The required quantity of metal used was important for the founder in view of the cost of bronze, particularly in the case of large objects such as weapons or bells. The danger that, in the end, he might have insufficient molten metal, forced the masters to work with a reserve of material, as this would greatly complicate or even ruin the entire work. For that reason, from the earliest time the medieval masters used exact methods of calculating the weight of metal needed, taking into account the weight of wax or clay needed for the model. They had at their disposal various tables to do so. The oldest is a table that gives the ratio of wax to metal which was compiled in the tenth century by Froumund, a monk in the Tegernsee monastery in Upper Bavaria. Froumund stipulated the ratio of wax to bronze at 1 : 8.5. Later in the Middle Ages, when it became customary to make clay models for larger objects, this ratio between metal and clay was usually stipulated at 7:1.

Another important task the founder had to perform was to anticipate the loss of metal caused by oxidation during the melting process. He had to take into account both the ratio between copper and tin in the melt and whether he was working with new raw material or using scrap metal. Biringuccio stated that a five to eight per cent loss had to be reckoned with, but to be certain to have sufficient material at their disposal the masters calculated on a ten per cent melting loss, since these were only rough estimates.

In order to ascertain the quantity required, the founder had to pay attention to the quality. He worked with two types of material. One type of material used was copper and tin bought on the market. Here, too, the master had to expect that the quality of the metal varied since it came from different mining areas and foundries. The second source of material were old, discarded objects, which very often formed a considerable part of the melt. Reports exist showing that members of a congregation collected bronze, copper and pewter vessels and tools so that a bell could be cast for their parish church. The founder had to stipulate the quality of all this material from what he knew on the basis of his own experiences. For instance, the grey, dull colour of a fracture in the bronze indicated a high lead or iron content; a smooth and silvery-white colour showed a high tin content; the fine-grained and dense structure of such a fracture was a guarantee of good quality bronze. The assessment of the starting material served him to determine the course of the casting and to decide what metal had to be added to the alloy to achieve the required quality of the new cast.

The culmination of all this preparatory work came with the casting itself, when the most important task rested firmly on the shoulders of the founder. The process of casting involved three main elements: the melt, the actual casting and the surface treatment of the cast. A decisive role towards the success of the melting process was played by the melting furnace. Virtually every author of a foundry handbook stresses that the furnace had to fulfil two basic conditions: the structure of the furnace had to be in proportion to the quantity and type of metal and it had to be constructed so as to melt the metal as easily as possible and could be maintained at the optimal temperature for casting. The functional efficiency of the furnace determined the success of casting. In the Middle Ages, in Europe, they used exclusively shaft furnaces, and only at the end of that period is there mention of reverberatory furnaces (e.g. in Lersner's Frankfurt Chronicle of 1486). For a shaft furnace to achieve the required heat quickly and evenly, a blower was an essential part of the furnace, similar in construction to the blacksmith's bellows. Metal nozzles ended inside the furnace and the bellows were attached to these from outside. The imput of air and its directions through the nozzles was determined by the master personally as he kept an eye on the melting process throughout.

The construction of a shaft furnace varied greatly. Theophilus, the monk, gave a detailed description of such a shaft furnace using an iron cauldron. The cauldron had to have a convex base and two handles opposite each other along the upper rim. The entire cauldron was set in clay and its stability was ensured along the

rim by wooden pegs driven into the ground. In the place where the air jets were to be, two poles were placed close to each other and a hole for the air vent was cut into them. A furnace of stone and loam was built around such a cauldron to reach one and a half feet above the upper rim of the cauldron with the required air vents left free. The inside of the cauldron and the walls of the furnace were lined with three layers of well mixed loam. Then the jets were attached and fixed to the bellows. Now the furnace was ready; all that remained to be done was to fire it with charcoal. When the metal compound was smelted the cauldron was pulled up by the handles, and the molten metal was poured into the prepared mould. Clearly the contents of one cauldron did not suffice for larger casts. Either the founder built several smaller furnaces side by side or he enlarged the cauldron to the required proportions. Then, of course, it was not possible to handle a large cauldron filled with molten metal. For that reason the iron cauldron was sometimes equipped with a tap hole and the base was not convex but slanted towards this tap hole. Such an iron cauldron was, however, not an essential part of a furnace. In the early Middle Ages there existed furnaces that were built only of masonry. The size of the furnace corresponded to the quantity of metal that the founder needed for one cast. We know of very small furnaces and also of others that reached to height of five metres.

From such shaft furnaces they derived a special type of furnace in a wicker basket. The founder, originally the bell-founder, often worked in the place where the order was placed. Sometimes it was not possible to build a masonry furnace there and so he had to make do with a very simple construction for a furnace. Poles rammed in the ground at the required distance, one from the other, were bound together with wicker so that a kind of basket resulted. The interior of this basket was lined with a thick layer of loam with a tap hole. When this had been fired with charcoal, the smelting device was ready. Such furnaces were of varying sizes.

Around the middle of the fifteenth century a new type of furnace began to appear, called reverberatory furnaces, in which the metal was separated from the fuel. This was an improvement that made

166 Forged door-lock of gilded bronze with the typical relief decorations of the late 18th century. Central Europe. Length 18 cm. Museum of Decorative Arts, Prague.

smelting easier. Such a furnace had as its basis a masonry structure built on a rectangular ground plan, in which there were two chambers. The smaller combustion chamber was divided by a low wall from the larger vaulted chamber, on the floor of which there was a shallow depression where the molten metal accumulated. There were various holes in the furnace walls which served for observation and servicing the smelt. During the construction of a reverberatory furnace the founder's full attention was centred on the correct proportion between the combustion and the smelting chamber. He was concerned that the entire charge should be heated as effectively and evenly as possible without great heat loss. In the initial period, the fifteenth century, it was thought that the best ground plan for a smelting chamber was the circle while an oval was popular for the combustion chambers. Before long, however, oval smelting chambers began to appear. Sometimes there were two combustion chambers. There existed a number of different forms, but the basic construction remained unchanged.

Now let us see what the founder did during the course of the smelting, first in a shaft furnace. To begin with, the furnace had to be properly heated, so the furnace-man placed large pieces of charcoal on the bottom, which he heated up red hot with the aid of bellows. When the charcoal was hot, he placed on it the material for the smelt and covered it with a layer of small pieces of charcoal and again used the bellows to heat everything up until the material began to melt. Then he placed another layer of charcoal on it and again material for smelting and continued doing this until he had a sufficient quantity of molten metal.

In the case of reverberatory furnaces the process differed. The material, in the first place, could not be placed on the bottom of the furnace but on a supporting grate at the height of about a quarter of an ell so that the hot material should not lose heat on the bottom of the furnace and so that the flames had free access to it from all sides. The bronze-founder first placed copper into the furnace and once it was perfectly smelted added the tin. It was a sign of the founder's skill to know the exact moment when the tin had to be placed on the smelted copper. If this was not done at the right moment, the smelting loss tended to be great. He also had to have sufficient quantity of smelted copper as any later addition to this copper again increased the loss. One further danger lurked for the inexperienced furnaceman if he placed old copper pots, goblets, jugs and cups into the smelt without previous treatment. These small objects would drop to the bottom, not quite smelted, merge together and the remnants thus created could not be liquified even during a prolonged smelting period. It was, therefore, recommended that these objects should be smelted first and alloyed in a smaller shaft furnace and used for the main smelt in that form.

The moment of casting slowly approached. First it was necessary to test the quality of the alloy. This was usually done by having a sample of the molten metal poured on the floor, left to cool and then broken up. The colour and density of the alloy could be tested on the fracture, and this revealed its quality. If everything was in order, casting could begin. It was of basic importance to ensure that the metal was poured into the mould slowly to give the air time to escape from the mould and for the metal to settle evenly into it. This required the flow of the metal to have sufficient pressure to extrude the air. The experience of the founder, who had to check the impact of the flow of metal was decisive here. When the metal appeared at the tap hole the founder paused for a moment until the level dropped and the mould could be filled.

There were different views as to when the mould should be removed to reveal the cast. It seems that in the early Middle Ages the metal-founder removed the mould as soon as possible, which, according to Theophilus, contributed to the hardening of the cast. With the passing of time the view dominated that the cast should be left a sufficiently long time in the mould to mature. Cooling depended on the size of the cast. Not until he removed the mould did the master see his work and was able to judge how successful it was and only at this point did the tension in the workshop relax. The cast still needed finishing surface treatment.

167 Examples of mounts from the end of the 18th century, made almost in series either by casting brass or pressing brass sheet. Central Europe. Height *c.* 7 cm. Museum of Decorative Arts, Prague.

168 Two gilded brass knobs as often found on furniture drawers at the turn of the 18th to 19th century. Central Europe. Largest diameter 6.5 cm. Museum of Decorative Arts, Prague.

Vessels had, in the first place, to be turned on the lathe. The technology of turning metal vessels on a wooden core was known in ancient Rome from the fourth century B.C. Most of the Roman metal vessels were made in this manner before being exported to the countries north of the Alps. This technology was not forgotten after the fall of the Roman Empire and continued to be used in European workshops. It reached great perfection in Germany at the end of the fifteenth century. Nuremberg brass products were valued as they were exceptionally light and this was achieved by excellent turning. W. Stengel published the organization of the work of the Nuremberg brassmakers, and it may be of interest to recall certain facts. The turner's workshops were concentrated around four mills, whose water power turned the lathes. There were about thirty workshops and the manner of work and construction of the lathes was a strict secret. Every founder-brazier had his own turner, with whom he permanently collaborated and who had to give priority to the orders of his master. There were money premiums for turning an object, calculated according to the weight of the waste chips. This measure was to encourage the turner to carry out perfect work and save material since the Nuremberg brass-makers had mainly to rely on fragments of old brass objects for their production. It would be a waste of time to identify the brass alloys in the case of old Nuremberg works since one smelt differed from another.

Other surface treatment on bronze or brass casts included tooling, a technique already known to the Mesopotamian founders. In this final treatment of the raw cast they were the direct ancestors of the Greek bronze-founders, who did not regard a bronze cast as finished until its surface had been tooled. Ancient tooling consisted of finishing the details and treating the surface with the aid of various chisels, rasps and graters. In accordance with the ancient concept of beauty the founder made efforts to raise the effect of its qualities. He, therefore, used various materials to improve the polish, and graving chisels and punches to adjust the details of the relief. Tooling also removed possible faults in the cast. Through this work the cast became an original and lost

169 Horse harness decoration in the shape of a comb with relief figures at the top. Cast brass. Probably Nuremberg, before mid 19th century. Museum of Decorative Arts, Prague.

the character of mechanical reproduction. Tooling was raised to an art form again in eighteenth century France.

The art-loving and cultured French of the time knew how to value the artistic contribution of tooling to the general effect of a work of art and the name of the chisellers tended to be given beside that of the sculptors, model-makers and ebenists. In addition, chiselling was required in modelling the mould for a bronze or brass cast. Among famous craftsmen we again encounter names known from earlier chapters, e.g. Jacques Caffieri, P. Gouthière and P. Ph. Thomire.

The fame of French chisellers spread across Europe. Some English producers sent raw bronze or brass casts to be tooled in France, and work on the Bronze Hall at the Town Palace at Potsdam was entrusted to a Frenchman called Geoffroy. Chisellers from France were summoned also to other German towns, among them to the château at Ansbach where a chiseller named Houdon worked around the middle of the eighteenth century.

Until the middle of the nineteenth century, Europe could not do without the skill of French masters. The German sculptor Gottfried Schadow, without hesitation, invited founder Lequine and chiseller Coué from Paris in 1818 to work on a bronze monument to Blücher in Rostock and his disciple Christian Rauch entrusted the chiselling of a Blücher monument at Breslau to the Frenchman Vuarin, who also worked on the monument of Maximilian IV Joseph in Munich in 1830. In 1824 in Berlin a special School of Chiselling was set up within the School of Artistic Metal-Casting, and M. Coué of France was put in charge. The school did not exist for long, Ch. Rauch recommended that the students should go to Paris to train.

The same is true of other countries in the early nineteenth century, for instance, Scandinavia and Russia and the countries in the Austro-Hungarian Empire, where metal casting skills were acquired from France or through the mediation of Germany.

Another important surface treatment of bronze and brass was gilding. In Antiquity both fire gilding and gilding with gold foil were known.

Fire gilding through the use of an amalgam of mercury and gold gave permanence to the surface and a lovely golden colour. It was colour-fast so that gilded objects did not go black. Since the gilding had to be repeated several times and the escaping mercury vapour was poisonous it is not surprising that gilding by fire was very expensive. Gilding of bronze and brass assumed special importance in seventeenth and eighteenth century France, especially on objects decorating the interior of buildings and on furniture mounts. This process was called 'doré d'or molu'. This gave rise to the term 'ormolu' or 'ormuli' throughout Europe, referring to gilt bronze and gilding of substitute alloys. In view of the cost of gilding most of the

202

bronze or brass objects were protected from atmospheric effects by the use of a far cheaper lacquer, which was made to stress their golden colour. An interesting formula for preparing such lacquer, dating from the middle of the nineteenth century, has been published by G. Wills. This is four parts of shellac, gamboge, and dragon blood, warmed and mixed with one part of saffron and twenty-five parts of pure alcohol. The saffron and gamboge (gum from the tropical Garcinia hauberrgi tree) served as yellow colouring matter, and the dragon blood was a reddish, resinous substance won from various tropical plants.

In conclusion, mention should be made of patinating bronze objects. The patina of new era bronze is the result of a misunderstanding dating back to ancient Rome. The Roman collectors of Greek bronzes judged the age of a statue of an object by its patina and thereby its genuinessness. The Greeks, however, valued bronze because of its polish and golden colour and for religious treasures they coated their statues with oil which prevented the emergence of patina. In France, at the same time when everybody was enchanted with excavations in Pompeii, they imitated the patina of objects found, quite intentionally, even on furniture mounts and decorations. This surface treatment was known as 'verde antique'.

170 Wicker furnace. Reproduction from the book by V. Biringuccio *De la pirotechnia libri X* (first edition 1540).

Copper Mills

Hammer for forging bases.

Copper mills were an important connecting link between craftsmen making various objects of copper and smelting plants that smelted raw copper from the ore. The mills produced copper plate for further treatment, and sheets, rods, wire and later circular disks, slightly thickened in the middle for the production of the base of vessels as well as various rough-forged vessels of different sizes. The mills were basically large smithies, in which raw copper from the smelting plant was worked with heavy hammers, generally using water power. To give a clearer picture it can be shown that the mill at Banská Bystrica, in the centre of rich deposits of copper in what is now Slovakia and was then Upper Hungary, was set up at the end of the fifteenth century by the Thurse-Fugger Mining Company. It had three large and three small hammers moved by five water-wheels. Copper was smelted or preheated on thirteen fireplaces with ten water-wheels. The mill produced roofing sheets and copper wire. Attached to the

mill was a workshop making copper vessels, which annually from the sixteenth to eighteenth century used between twelve and twenty nine tons of copper. Most of the products were intended for long-distance trade.

Copper was brought to the mill in the form of large chunks of metal of varying weight. This raw material was suitable for those crafts that had to remelt it, such as bronze, brass and bell-makers. But it was too fragile and soft for hammering. The mills had the task of adapting the raw foundry copper so as to make it malleable. This was achieved most easily by re-smelting and with the addition of old used copper. After two to three hours the mill worker would take a little of the melted copper on a pole, let it cool and work it with a hand hammer to find out whether cracks had formed during forging and whether it was sufficiently ductile. After this cold test a second one followed, forging in a hot state, this time treating metal cooled to the red stage with a water ham-

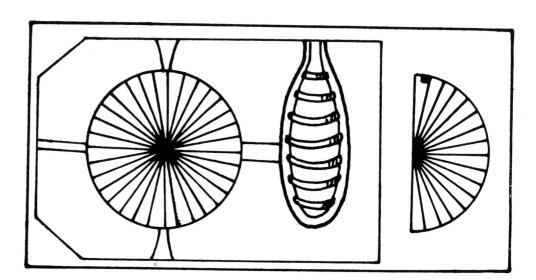

171 Plan of a circular furnace. Reproduced from the book by V. Biringuccio *De la pirotechnia libri X* (first edition 1540).

mer. When the copper was regarded in proper condition the finished copper was tapped into a special vessel holding fifty six pounds.

For the forging of copper three types of hammers were required; a broad hammer to forge sheets, a depth hammer for forging bases and a polishing hammer for the ultimate finish of copper plate and sheet. Each type of hammer needed a different type of anvil. Anvils for forging copper could not be fixed into hard ground or on a solid base since the soft metal, forged into plate or sheet, would easily have been pierced under the strokes of the steel hammer and would have been spoilt. For that reason an anvil was sunk into the ground on a layer of brushwood and branches of hard wood, mostly oak, which did not rot in the ground. The brushwood fulfilled the function of making the entire anvil spring-mounted.

Other important equipment in the copper mills included stamps, which cut up the clinkers of melted copper. These stamps were mostly run by water-wheels. The crushed clinkers fell from the stamp into a large boiler sunk into the ground into which water was steadily running. The larger pieces of copper that the clinker still contained sank to the bottom of the boiler while the lighter clinkers were carried off by the water.

The copper mills produced copper plate and sheet as their basic products and, among others, pot bases. The plate was formed by the mill-worker guiding the strokes of the water-hammer into a piece of copper in parallel manner side by side in dense rows. When he reached the end of the piece being forged he turned it so that the next row of strokes should run perpendicular to the preceding direction. To make it even everywhere the strokes were directed more closely or the number of strokes was reduced in places. Small plates were made by one worker alone. Large-sized plates needed up to four assistants.

Thin copper sheets were forged in a dif-

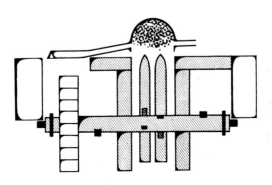

Construction of the stamp for crushing clinker in a copper mill.

ferent manner. First, the worker forged relatively thick sheets from individual pieces of copper so that the strokes on the thick sheet should not cause damage to hammer and anvil and then they were cut to an even size. The individual sheets of the plate were placed one on top of the other, about eight at a time, and this bunch was heated in the hearth. It was very important that all the sheets in the bunch should be evenly heated. Then the entire bunch was forged together. This process was repeated until the individual layers were fairly thin. If the worker wanted even thinner plate he bent the bundle in half as one does with paper. He then placed a double number of layers of plate under the hammer and thus forged them very thin.

The master coppersmith had to pay greatest attention to forging the base of pots. First, a circular disc had to be forged from a piece of copper. Then it had to be forged to make sure that the centre was thicker than the edges so that it was in the end shaped like a split pea. The coppersmith then led the hammer from the edge to its centre and keeping a steady eye on the edge since the soft copper might easily fracture there. Any crack had to be cut off immediately to prevent it spreading further. Finished bases were piled one on top of the other. Large ones, intended as the bottom of vessels the size of a copper for boiling linen, were piled up in ten to twenty pieces, the smaller ones per twenty. The

bottom one had to be the widest so that its edge could be bent over the others. Such a bundle was further heated in the hearth and when hot the coppersmith began to forge them. With a few strokes of the water-hammer he thrust the individual pieces close to make sure they would not fall out of the bundle. Then the actual forging began. To achieve the required convexity he led the strokes of the water-hammer from the centre to the edge while turning the bases clockwise. The whole bundle had to be kept heated in the hearth.

To make sure that even the concave bottom was heated through, the bundle was placed into the hearth upside down, i.e. with the concave part at the top and the vessel without a bottom was placed on top, filled with hot coal. Even with the greatest care and attention the top and bottom parts often cracked during forging. They were set aside once the work was finished and added to the scrap for re-use. The coppersmith used special pliers to hold the pieces under the water-hammer: they had one straight gripping jaw and one with a mighty curve. When the pieces were forged to the required shape, their edges were cut to make them straight, and they were smoothed with a wooden hammer. At the very end they were heated once again and quickly submerged in cold water so that they should lose their blackened appearance and regain the colour of copper.

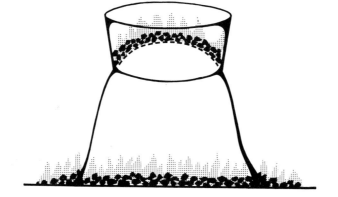

Heating the convex base of a vessel prior to further forging.

The Coppersmith's Workshop

The workshop of the coppersmith used to be equipped with tools and instruments that can be divided into two basic groups: anvil, hammer, tongs and various tools such as scissors, saws, drills etc. Let us take a brief look at the tools typical of a coppersmith's trade and the specific tasks for which they were used.

There were two types of large anvils, one for working copper in a hot state, the other for working in cold. The basic type of anvil for working in the hot state had a narrow work-top, about 7 by 10 cm wide, which did not greatly differ from a blacksmith's anvil, another type had a much broader but shorter work-top. This broad anvil was typical of the coppersmith's workshop. When he worked copper cold he usually had at his disposal three types of anvils: one with a convex work-top and concave sides narrowing downwards, another with a straight top, rectangular in shape with sides that broadened in convex manner downwards, and lastly an anvil in the shape of a cube with a flat work-top with edges 25 to 35 cm in length. All these anvils could be moved.

173 Seal of the Brno guild of copper-makers. The inscription on the frieze around the edge reads 'SIGIL DES LOBLICHEN HANTWERCK D KUPFERSCHMIE IN D KONIGSDAT BRIN 1664'. Diameter 4.2 cm. Archives of the City of Brno.

Horizontal anvil fixed to a block of hard wood.

Various types of anvils used in a coppersmith's workshop.

174 Brass Saturday candlestick in the shape of a double-headed eagle. The oval breastplate of the eagle has a star of David engraved into it. Poland, first half of 19th century. Height 40.5 cm. State Jewish Museum, Prague.

Various types of small anvils.

The most widely used and therefore most typical contrivances in the coppersmith's workshop were the horizontal anvils. These were tetragonal iron poles, usually 5 cm wide and 120—150 cm long, with both ends broadening to form anvils of varying shape. The shape depended on the kind of work for which they were used. These horizontal anvils were fixed to a block of hard wood, mostly oak, cut just above the root to be highly resistant and tough. This block was firmly built into the workshop floor. A workshop had several such blocks. They were roughly 100 cm high with a slot into which the horizontal anvils were placed and attached on both sides with triangular wooden wedges widening downwards. To provide as great a variety of such anvils as possible some of the horizontal anvils had a square hole at one end, into which smaller anvils of different shapes could be affixed. These attachable anvils were called 'fists', and each coppersmith's workshop had a large supply of such fists, as they were essential in hammering vessels.

For forging very large coppers and pots a special tool was used. It was made from a twisted tree trunk, at one end a square swage was cut, lined with metal foil and held fast from the outside with a metal strip into which attachable anvils were placed, shaped according to need. Similarly for forging the base of larger vessels they used a standing anvil, about 100 cm high, made from an iron pillar with a widening rounded top.

Essential for work on the anvil was the hammer and its shape was determined by its use. There were hammers to expand or draw together copper plate and sheet, to gouge and smooth, for inserting wire into the rim of vessels, for cutting the base of coppers and pots, and for removing the flange. There were polishing hammers, which had to have such a mirror-like work-edge that they were made with a fine file and polished with slate and Viennese lime. Another tool that was widely used in the coppersmith's workshop was the mallet, its shape again differing according to need. The mallet used for hammering the base differed in shape from that used for working the sides, etc. Such a mallet for hammering vessels and deep pots was some 50 cm long or even longer and for hammering the base of ves-

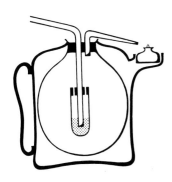

Fan of poultry feathers used to direct the flame to the brazed place.

Predecessor of the present-day soldering torch, the mercury blow-pipe.

sels sometimes metal poles ending in a wooden block were needed. This was usually of hornbeam wood, which was exchanged once it wore out.

Other essential tools were tongs. Apart from normal tongs used in every smithy, like pincers, forge tongs, wire-pliers, the coppersmith, in addition, needed specially shaped tongs for his work. For example, there were tongs for the crucible from which solder was poured, tongs to hold products for soldering and tongs with which wire was placed into the rim of the vessels. Each one was adapted to ease work, and the shape differed according to local or even workshop custom.

Essential jobs of the coppersmith included brazing and soldering, which was linking metal sheets by solder. Heat of varying intensity was essential, for brazing depended on the size of the joint. For that reason some old depictions of coppersmiths show him using bellows to blow the flame of a candle onto the soldered place. A stand was used to fix the candle and the soldered object and the level of the candle or object could be altered. But far more often, they used coal to produce heat and the flame could be blown on to the brazed place in two ways, either with bellows or a tool resembling a fan. This was usually a bird or poultry feather fixed onto a handle. The master's assistant made rapid movements to direct the flame to the brazed place. An apparently slight movement of the feather fan became hard work causing the wrists to swell when the brazing involved large areas, and the assistant had to wave his fan for several hours on end.

Some time before the middle of the nineteenth century there appeared, in Germany, the predecessor of the present-day soldering torch: the mercury blow pipe. Basically, this was a glass flask with two tubes in its neck, one used for the intake of air and the other as outlet. For the flask to stand up to the pressure of the air achieved by breathing into it, the end of the inlet tube inside the flask was submerged in a receptacle with mercury. The outlet of the air was regulated with a finger placed on the narrower pointed tube. One proper breath sufficed for two minutes of brazing, with the outlet of air to the brazed object coming continuously and relatively evenly. The majority of master coppersmiths made their own devices so that we can find different shapes and improvements, but the technical basis is always the same.

Making Copper Vessels

Nowadays, copper utensils serve as decorations and few cooks now use them. Yet copper pots and moulds were once an integral part of kitchen equipment and the pride of every housewife.

Until the end of the last century, copper vessels and moulds were made by hand in coppersmiths' workshops. Every master coppersmith had a sufficient quantity of copper material and half-finished products as described in the chapter on the work of the copper mills. The production of copper vessels was time-consuming except in the case of the simplest things such as pots, baking tins, baking sheets, frying pans, etc.; it required skill and experience and, in many cases, artistic feeling.

Commonplace vessels of large size such as sinks for washing dishes, pots and kettles were made of copper sheets of the required thickness, to which a base was brazed and a simple lid or handle attached. Smaller objects, drinking cups, ladles, small pots etc. were forged out of one piece. The master also used one piece to make kettles suspended on a chain over the fire as well as cauldrons on three legs to be placed into the hearth.

Baking tins were hammered either from oval bases or sheet metal, cut into an oval in shape. At the ends, the sheet was cut to the assumed height of the walls of the dish, the edge was turned up and all was soldered together. Often the rim was reinforced with wire to make it firmer. To cover the wire, the rim was made two and a half times wider than its diameter. If the master had made the rim shorter, the wire would not have been fully covered, if it was wider, folds would have resulted that it would have been difficult to remove by hammering.

True masterpieces which proved the coppersmith's skill were richly decorated baking utensils of various shapes and appearance. Copper sheet, generally 1 to 2 mm thick, was used for these. The thickness of the sheet depended on the size of the object to be made and the wish of the client; heavier objects of thicker metal were regarded as of higher quality. They were also more expensive, since the price was fixed according to the weight. A base was made in the shape of the future vessel and it was filled with melted resin. Once the resin hardened, the metal was turned

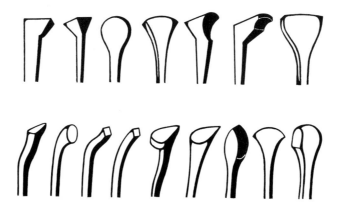

Various types of anvils used for hammering shapes, ornaments and patterns on copper vessels and baking tins.

176 Set of children's cups and plates from the first half of the 19th century. These toys were exact copies of contemporary household utensils. Central Europe. Height of pot 2.5 cm. National Museum, Prague.

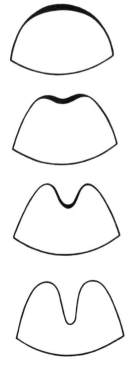

Sequence of work in hammering a cake tin from one piece of copper plate.

out on the work-table and work on the decorations could begin. The master would draw a pattern from the centre to the edge. More highly skilled masters used their imagination to draw their patterns straight onto the metal, others first drew the future decorations on paper. This was then cut out and stuck with glue made of water and rye flour. When the glue had dried, they copied the pattern from this and marked bulges and depressions.

The resinous substance had to be sufficiently strong and, at the same time, elastic to adjust to the hammered pattern. If the future form was not filled with resin, the pattern was hammered only in flat relief and only after removing the resin from the form could the coppersmith attain the pattern in its definitive sharpness of edges and required depth. This final hammering was carried out with small hammers on tiny anvils.

In workshops where pastry cutters were produced in large quantities and the cus-

tomers preferred certain types of decorations, work was made easier and speeded up by using stamping dice in the shape of the main decorative features, such as flowers, leaves, branches, hearts, stars, crosses, fish scales, geometrical patterns etc. The contours of the whole range of prepared ornamental features were impressed on the metal filled with resin and new combinations gave rise to new variations of ornaments. On the little anvils they then hammered both the definitive depth of the reliefs and the links between twigs, flowers, tendrils etc.

Cake tins were more complicated, particularly for cakes that enjoyed popularity in Central Europe. Originally such cake tins were made without a central 'funnel' so that these tins did not greatly differ from others, but some time around the eighteenth century a central hollow cone appeared in the middle of this type of cake tin, reaching in height to the edge of the tin. In the early days, until the beginning of the nineteenth century, such a cake tin was made of one piece. The circular piece of copper, from which it was made, had to have a thick centre to ensure there would be enough metal to draw up the central funnel. Compasses were used to mark the circle wider than the future diameter of this funnel. The edges of the metal were heated by stages, and when

211

hot, the sides of the future tin were drawn out. When the sides were ready, the master drew out the central funnel from the thicker metal in the centre. When he reached the required height he lopped off the top to enable hot air to pass through it.

Cake tins that had the central funnel soldered on were made by first forging the complete shape without this central funnel, for which insufficient material was left in the centre. Then the tin was filled with pitch, spread along the entire circumference where relief ornaments were to be made and these were first carried out only in a shallow manner. Then a chisel was used to make a hole for the funnel in the centre. Once it was soldered, the edges of the cake tin were cleaned up, wire was applied to reinforce the rim and it was attached. Then the whole tin was annealed anew and the pattern was hammered on the anvils into its final shape.

In other words, the production of such cake tins involved demanding and time-consuming work. Reports show that most of the copper cake tins with rich ornaments were made by skilled and experienced masters or journeymen, and the work took them two full days. It has been calculated that some thirty thousand strokes of the hammer were needed to complete such a cake tin. Care had to be

taken so that no folds or flat areas emerged in the pattern which would prevent the smooth turn-out of the finished cake. The price of such cake tins with rich ornamentation was usually fixed according to the weight of the object, without much regard to the work involved in making the decorations. For that reason the price was not much higher than that of a simple copper vessel.

The coppersmith used different methods to produce small and delicate objects. The basic preparation involved a hemisphere of putty resting on a leather wreath filled with sawdust so that it could be freely turned and twisted without moving. The upper part of this hemisphere was covered with a special mixture of pitch. For instance a mixture of three parts of pitch, two parts of brick dust and one part of coal dust was used. Of course, there existed a large number of different recipes for such mixtures, varying from region to region, locality or town and even individual workshops. The object to be made was first slightly heated so as to adhere to the pitch mixture fairly firmly so that it would not move during work. In hammering patterns the coppersmith used the same process as for cake tins. He first drew the riquired pattern and then with the aid of hammers and various dies applied it. From time to time he heated the stone base slightly to keep the pitch mixture elastic and flexible so that the hammered metal should easily press into it. For larger bulges he removed the object, heated it and attached it anew to the hemisphere.

When a small hollow object had to be made the coppersmith used a different process. He first filled the object with heated liquid putty, then he heated this putty on the hemisphere with a piece of hot coal from the furnace where he wished to attach the object on hand. He had to work very fast so that the pitch mixture poured into the hollow object should not go cold and to ensure the object adhered well to the putty sphere. Hollow objects which were too large to attach to the putty sphere had to be affixed for hammering in a different manner. First they were filled with a liquid mixture of pitch, and while still hot, an iron rod was placed into this. Once the putty cooled and hardened the rod could be fixed into a vice. The coppersmith had to be especially careful once the hollow object was

177 Copper pot with spout, lid and two handles. Example of good quality work of a coppersmith around the mid 19th century. Bohemia. Height excluding lid 23 cm. Museum of the City of Prague.

178 Detail showing how the iron handle was attached to a copper pot. Second half of 18th century.

finished. The putty had to be heated and poured out of the object. The whole thing was heated over a hot charcoal fire and when the mixture was poured out of the object, not a drop of the putty was allowed to fall into the fire, since the flame which the putty caused would give the copper a black smudge that was difficult to remove. For that reason they never used an open fire to remove the remnants of putty from inaccessible places but used hot oil.

The master coppersmith was expected to have a knowledge of colouring copper products, which was often demanded for decorative or representative objects, e.g.

coffee or teapots. Here are some examples taken from the memoirs of an old master. Brown-coloured copper was popular and to achieve this, ferric oxide was used with Venetian red and purple brown, which were mixed with water to form a thick cream and then coated on the object with a brush. Then it was heated in the fire until the coat dried. When cool, the superfluous powder of the colouring matter was removed. According to another recipe, four half ounces of red caput mortuum or other ferric dyes were mixed with one half ounce of antler filings, ground to powder, and two ounces of finely ground verdigris in a little vinegar. Ox blood was also used for dyeing. The object was firstly carefully cleaned with fine ash and then rubbed with a weak solution of nitric acid. Dried ox blood was sprinkled on the bottom of the vessel that was used for dyeing. The object was hung into this receptacle, then placed on the fire and covered with a perforated lid for the vapour of the ox blood to escape. When this vapour ceased to rise, the object was removed and left to cool and after adding another lot of ox blood the process was repeated for as long as was necessary for the object to acquire the required tone.

The production of large copper vessels for craftsmen was a major source of income for the coppersmith. But the hand forging of a seamless copper using only a mallet, required both great experience and skill, certainty of stroke and involved great physical exertion. It was work for a master and one apprentice for two or three full days. Later manufacturers supplied half-finished products of such coppers, which eased work so that within the same span of time the master, aided by an apprentice, managed to make up three such vessels. Regular supplies included coppers of normal size, holding about 50 litres and larger or special coppers were made only on order.

Coppers were produced either from one circular sheet of metal or from casing and base. If made in one piece the base was forged on a convex steel anvil, about 20 cm in diameter. Wooden mallets were used for this work. The copper sheet was continually annealed. Usually it had to be heated four times before the required shape was attained. During the fifth annealing the rim was forged and after the sixth the edge was prepared for the inser-

179 Wick snuffers were a typical produce of brass-makers. These three examples were made by Bohemian or Prague brassmakers at the end of the 18th and in the early 19th century. Length of the smallest 6.5 cm. Museum of the City of Prague.

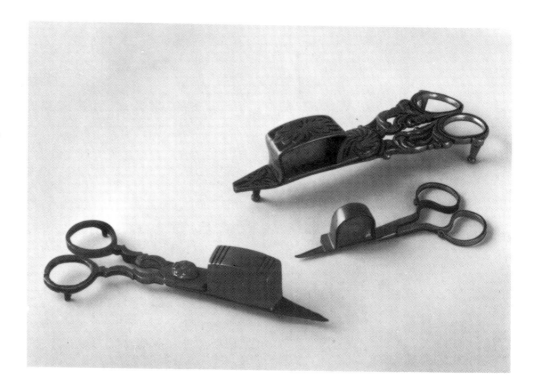

Sequence of work in hammering a cake tin with a soldered funnel.

Shape of a copper used for dyeing.

tion of an iron reinforcement along the rim. If such a copper was made of two parts, casing and base, a straight and rectangular piece of copper sheet was cut, which was forged to be wider and thinner at the top and narrower and thicker at the bottom. When copper was cheap, the master cut a length of copper sheet 1—1.5 mm thick to the required curvature. Casing and base were then brazed together.

For certain crafts the coppers had to be entirely hand forged even when there existed sufficient half-finished products. For dyeing, a deep copper was in demand with strong sides since the dye solution with acid reaction soon corroded them. There was also a demand for a round shape with a narrow neck so that the solution should not splash out of the copper. On the other hand, pastry-cooks wanted a copper solely in the shape of a hemisphere in which they could whip cream and white of eggs. Brewers requested coppers of the strongest metal to boil pitch for their barrels, for the hot pitch would otherwise quickly corrode the copper.

In conclusion mention should be made of tin-coating copper objects, which was of great importance for kitchenware. The object was first pickled in vinegar and salt or salt and cream of tartar to remove oxides that arose in the course of annealing the copper. Smaller objects that were to be completely tin-costed were submerged in a vat of melted tin. When tin-coating larger objects, the relevant part was first heated, then strewn with powdered tin or rubbed with a tin stick and on the heated walls the liquid metal would be spread with an oakum wick.

Collectors and Forgeries

Forgery of works of art and antiques goes back to ancient times. It is known that forgeries already existed in Antiquity and were produced for Roman lovers of Greek art. In the Middle Ages art forgery declined, with a shift to literary forgeries. They reappeared in larger numbers during the Renaissance since the relatively small number of existing works of Antiquity could not satisfy the interest of a new type of art lover, the collector. A new wave of forgeries emerged in the second half of the nineteenth century. This rise was related to the predominant attitude to art of the time, Historicism, when many newly rich people wished to add prestige to their homes by furnishing them with antique furniture and all the required fittings. Soon the supply of original works on the antique market could no longer satisfy demand and forgers had a great opportunity. Fakes from all spheres of the arts and crafts from all periods came into being.

These included forgeries of bronze, brass and copper objects. These fakes present a major problem for the collectors who want to enlarge their collection, particularly if less experienced. There is no entirely reliable way to recognize a forgery. In examining a doubtful object, systematic attention needs to be paid to one aspect after the other. Here are some brief suggestions of what to do when examining an object of interest to the collector and some principles that every collector should adhere to.

Collectors need to have a basic knowledge of specialist literature, not only recent publications but also older works that can serve as source material. In the first place, old catalogues of public and private collections, museum catalogues, monographs on various collections and auction catalogues. It is equally important for the collector to have a knowledge of the production processes. Also essential is knowledge of the history of art, aesthetics, archaeology, ethnography, etc. according to the nature of the collection. Without this background the collecting of antiques is out of the question. The collector needs also to be acquainted with such fields as

180 Jug of copper plate adorned with hammered floral decoration. Central Europe, first half of 18th century. Height 41.5 cm. Museum of the City of Prague.

215

181 Copper barrel with a hammered scene of a coppersmith's workshop. Dated 1899. Property of the Prague Community of Coppersmiths. Height 11.5 cm. Museum of the City of Prague.

heraldry, palaeography, sphragistics, numismatics and others. The main task of a collector is to identify an object, that is to fit it into its time and determine its region or place of origin.

In examining an object it should be approached without preconceived ideas as though one did not know anything about it. In practice that means nobody else's attribution should be taken into account, no expert opinion by a merchant, no written attribution, etc. At this point it is decisive that no analysis should be made and no criticism of other people's opinion be put forward. This should be left to the very

end. The actual attribution of an object has two main parts, one direct, one indirect. Direct attribution is based on the object itself in that it deals with the style in which it is made and the technical level of artistic treatment. It also concerns the material of which the object is made. It is based on the shape of the object, which is a fairly safe guideline and, using this, we then try to determine the time of origin. A further step is to find out the country or region where the object originated, and this requires more detailed knowledge. First, try to compare the piece with similar pieces of known regional styles. This will be much easier if it is an object with a specific purpose used in a certain region or country. In some cases it will be possible to find the closest place of origin or even workshop of a master craftsman according to the composition of the object, its shape, certain technology used in making it or even the character of the treatment, though this is rare in our case.

Such a comparison requires the collector to know as many objects in his field as possible and to have an idea of the period at least from pictures. Most important are the experiences that a collector gains with direct observation. Details that a photograph cannot reproduce can reveal a great deal and can be used for attribution. In the first place, the manner of production, the tools used in surface treatment, the manner of chasing and varnishing, the patina and its type, etc. All of this can be imitated but only with difficulty.

Once you have exhausted all the possibilities of gaining information from the work itself, try to turn to subsidiary reports on the object. In the first place, information on its history, the place where it originated, which collections it belonged to, whether it was sold by auction, etc. An object with definitive locality or from a serious collection can be assumed not to be a forgery or copy. At that point, sum up all facts ascertained. By comparison of the two spheres of judgment, your own art historical analysis of the object and the result of the study of historical sources it is often possible to decide with certainty whether you are dealing with an original object, a copy or even a forgery.

Such direct attribution is, however, rather rare, particularly in the case of objects made of bronze, brass or copper, especially if you are dealing with objects of daily use. This requires an analysis of the technical aspects. In decorative work, particularly where the surface has been tooled, the best guideline is to look for the craftsmen's tools. These must be compared with other guaranteed old objects. Here experience gained by study in museums or accessible private collections will be of great help. Another important point in determining the age of an object is its patina. Casts of old works and objects made by the 'creative' phantasy of a forger are exposed to various procedures and methods to acquire a patina, which, at first sight, would not rouse doubts.

By way of illustration here are some old recipes of how to artificially achieve a patina on objects of brass or bronze. The bronzes were washed and rubbed with oil or submerged in an acid solution with salt or extracts from plants. Most often a bath of diluted wine vinegar was used, and the object was exposed to the influence of carbon dioxide for some weeks. To forge patina on ancient bronzes the object was rubbed several times with a brush dipped in a solution of 4.5 parts of sal-ammoniac, 1 part of oxalate salt and 94.5 parts of vinegar. Shades of patina on bronze could also be achieved by submersion for a long time, often up to 64 hours, in a bath made up of 20 parts of castor oil, 80 parts of ethyl alcohol, 20 parts of Venetian soap and 40 parts of water. Patina could also be imitated by varnishing, using, for instance, light sandarac varnish mixed with a little copper hydroxide carbonate.

The greenish-brown patina on brass can be achieved by cleaning the object and placing it for a few seconds into a solution of 10 g of ammonium sulphate in 5 litres of water thickened with potassium lye. Then the object is submerged in water weakly acidified with sulphuric acid. Copper objects acquire a patina in the same process.

These few examples suffice to show that there exists a broad range of materials that forgers have been using. It is well to keep in mind that even forgers update their knowledge and materials. As a consequence it is very difficult to distinguish bronze, brass or copper forgeries. In the case of bronze or brass casts it is recommended that the colour of the metal be tested on a scratch and the ease of a cut on the edge be estimated, which, in new alloys, is greater than in old objects. The artificial patina, in some cases, appears more finely grained than true patina under a magnifying glass with greater magnifying capacity. The granulation of the patina on dull places should be irregular. These few steps tend to be imprecise as they are based on subjective impressions (ease with which scratches can be made) and cannot embrace the very broad range of technical and natural conditions under which a certain patina arose. Collectors can use their own experience in examining and attributing newly acquired objects. Four principles should be adopted.

182 Holy water font of copper plate. Such fonts, often also made of pewter, were usually to be found in households. Bohemia, second half of 18th century. Height 15.5 cm. Private collection, Prague.

1) Every object for testing should be approached with healthy doubt. Do not be influenced by various expert opinions, judgments or deductions, whether in writing or verbal. But it is important, and useful, if you know the 'genealogy' of the given object.

2) Try to gain precise information on the manner of production, treatment and ornamentation of objects of copper and its alloys. Here those collectors are at an advantage who concentrate on products of one type of material and one region, area or town. It is necessary to know some historical background, the first and last reports on production, guild organization and special, regional differences in production, and choice of ornamental motifs.

183   Coffee grinder of sheet brass. Central Europe, *c.* mid 19th century. Height 23 cm. Museum of the City of Prague.

Objects are often given names or associated with names or emblems of the original owner and here a knowledge of the history of the region is of great help. To be quite certain visit museum or good collections and study every detail on genuine objects from its shape to the colour of the alloy or metal and the way in which the tool was used in chasing or the graver in engraving ornaments. Only in this way can you train your eyes to recognize every detail.

3) It would be a grave mistake to rely only on intuition. In collecting, more than anywhere else, do not hurry to come to a conclusion since a hasty decision can be misleading. Impressions and conclusions must be constantly tested and the final judgment expressed only after thorough analysis of all criteria. Keep in mind that the forger or whoever copied the object also knew the manner of production and decoration of a certain period and a definite region.

4) In testing an object you must ultimately decide whether you are dealing with a forgery or a copy. It is necessary to work systematically from one aspect to the next, since it is highly likely that the forger or copyist did not have mastery of all production and ornamentation methods and may have made a mistake somewhere. In testing suspect objects follow this procedure:

a) Make a critical analysis of the material of which the object is made. A forger might have used older parts to which he added. A torso thus can become whole again, and such an object might fulfil its original function. Or the forger cast the original object and a combination of the old and new parts gave rise to two objects which are alleged to be the original ones. This is possible where parts of the objects are joined with screws and nuts as in the case of candlesticks. For that reason it is of basic importance that each part of the object be examined separately rather than making a superficial examination of the object as whole.

b) A popular method used by forgers to raise the price of an object is to add ornaments to an original piece, mainly in the form of engraving and figural motifs, to which the forger often adds the year to make the collector's work 'easier'. In the case of a suspect object, the ornaments need to be studied with several questions

218

184 Brass rulers. The twopartite one is the Vienna foot, divided on one side into 12 inches and 96 lines along the other. The year 1695 is punched on the ridge. The three-partite ruler is a yard-stick from the end of the 18th century. Bohemia or Austria. Museum of the City of Prague.

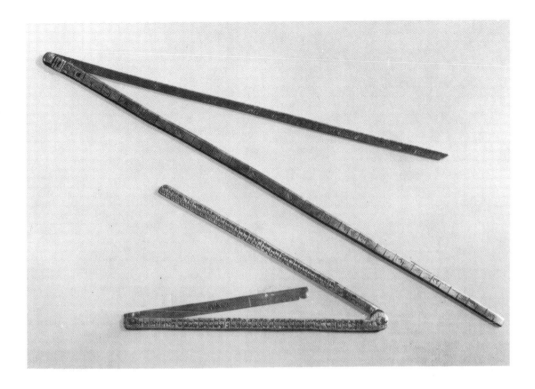

in mind. In the first place there is the matter of style, does its treatment and composition correspond to the period of which it is claimed to belong? This means making sure whether the decorative elements used (acanthus, rosettes, vine, tendrils, flower festoons, etc.) were used at the alleged time of origin. In the case of figural ornaments, check the garments of the figures, the hairstyle, and in particular the meaning of the scene and its iconography to make sure it corresponds to the typical manner in which such scenes were depicted at the time. Sometimes all that is needed is iconography of the depiction which may reveal a forgery.

c) In the case of objects hammered of sheet metal it is neccassary that you should know the technology of production and the marks that this leaves on the objects themselves. For instance, in the case of copper pastry cutters, hand made by using various types of hammers, the strokes of these tools are clearly visible to this day. Moulds pressed with steel stamps and polished by machines clearly have no such marks. But to complicate matters for the collector it should be said that sometimes machine-made moulds were finished with hammer strokes. In cast objects the surface can be given its final appearance by adapting it with the use of chisel, graver or file. Here, too, there exists period and regional differences, which you need to know and have to take into account in attributing an object.

d) It need not be stressed that you should keep an eye on new publications, should set up your own card file of suitable examples and remarkable objects, which can be used as comparative material and as information on prices. It is up to the collector himself that he should avail himself of all these aspects for his own advantage.

How to Look after Metal Objects

185   Two coffee machines of sheet brass. Central Europe, first half of 19th century. Height 42 cm. Museum of the City of Prague.

Every collector wants the things in his collection to be in good condition and protected from damage or destruction. Objects of copper, bronze or brass require far less care than those of other materials. Not even these are safe from the negative influences of the environment which — if exceeding a certain limit — can lead to the destruction of the object. Such negative influences emerge most strikingly in respect to unsuitable storage, which probably does not concern a purpose-built collection. The collector is more likely to acquire an object that is badly in need of attention to prevent its further gradual deterioration or to restore it to its original appearance. This involves two basic operations that must be distinguished: the preservation of the object and its restoration. Preservation means taking technical measures to make sure the object is in good condition so as to stop or slow down the disintegration of the basic material and keep it in its existing condition. Sometimes preservation is carried out as a prevention, that is, before the harmful processes rise to the fore. Correct preservation should be permanent and effective but should not change the appearance of the work of art.

Restoration is the renovation of the work; it is not limited to preservation but, in suitable manner, replaces small, missing or unessential parts. It involves many partial operations and technical and artistic measures. In other words, neither preservation nor restoration of objects is a simple matter, but require relatively extensive knowledge, and an untrained layman may, with the best will in the world, do a lot of harm to an object which can often be overcome only with difficulty. The restoration of an object, if essential, should be left to the expert who has more profound knowledge and the technical equipment at a more advanced level.

The simplest task is cleaning such an object. In the days when copper or brass vessels were part of every housewife's kitchenware the housewife knew many a recipe for cleaning and keeping it in good condition. Such recipes were in

220

186   Brass spice-box. The tin-covered interior is divided into several
compartments. Central Europe, *c.* mid 19th century. 15.5×10.5×7 cm.
Museum of the City of Prague.

cookery-books, calendars and booklets of
practical advice. M. Wiswe published
several such recipes, of which the most
interesting one is that recommending two
procedures, one German, the other
French.

According to the German recipe, the
object should be submerged into vinegar
water at a temperature of 50°C and then
dried and polished. The French method
recommends that the object be boiled in
water with lemon rind, then properly
rinsed in hot water and finally polished
with fine sand. Instructions for cleaning
objects of copper and its alloys in refer-
ence books for collectors published in the
1920s were still based on empirical experiences without making use of modern
chemistry. Here are some examples:

It is recommended that copper be
cleaned with a mixture of powder of stag
antlers, sheep bones or shells moistened in
alcohol with a little petrol.

Another mixture, recommended for
the cleaning of grass and copper, consists
of 240 g water, 15 g oxalacetic acid, 10 g
hydrogen oxide and 35 g floated whiting.

Another cleaning medium consists of
30 g sulphuric acid, 20 g pumice powder
and 200 g water. Soiled bronze, it is recommended, should be cleaned with
a boiling soap solution and then submerged in a bath with one part of concentrated nitric acid and 0.6 part of alum.

Most of the recipes recommend, for
polishing or cleaning, sand or pumice,
which is natural foam glass of volcanic
origin. If somebody wants to try out these
old recipes it should be done with the
greatest care so as not to spoil the surface
of the object by scratching it. Today we
know that the surface of old objects of
copper and its alloys is covered with a certain type of corrosion, from insignificant
coating to thick layers, which we call pat-

221

ina. We distinguish two kinds of patina, one noble, one wild. While the noble type protects the objects to a greater or lesser degree, is smooth and glass-like, does not alter the appearance of the object and does not destroy the ornamental engraving, the wild patina often penetrates deep into the material, deforms its appearance, destroys the shape and, chiefly, is a threat to the metal substance itself. These facts have to be borne in mind in caring for such objects. The noble patina should be cleaned only under running water and the grosser dirt should be carefully removed with a brush. But the wild patina should be removed from an object, paying atten-

tion, especially in the case of finds excavated from the ground, that the object should not be impaired once the thick layer of corrosion is removed. It should be realized that corrosion of various copper alloys may take different courses even if there is the same chemical or electrochemical base, i.e. the origin of copper oxide, hydrogen sulphide etc. Brass succumbs to dezincification and sponge-like copper is formed. Bronze is attached in the ground by extractive corrosion, i.e. the dissolution of copper, which penetrates into the surrounding ground. Bronze corrosion in the ground is highly complex since all aggressive elements in the surrounding soil attack it. Wild patina of copper and its alloys, which is the basic corroding threat, is formed by chloride anions.

The little excursion into chemistry, which does not encompass all the complexity of the problem, indicates that lay methods are far from sufficient in the case of serious threats to objects. The most effective stabilization of patina is carried out by an electrolytic conversion of chloride ions from a cathod to an anodic space or on a suitable ion exchanger. Naturally, only a well equipped specialist workshop will have such equipment at its disposal. The final treatment of preserved objects or preventive protection, if necessary, can be achieved with a surface coating. Formerly a saponine varnish used to be recommended, but this is not too suitable since, in time, it goes a striking yellow. Now acrylites are mostly used to varnish an object, they form a colourless and transparent coat on the surface of the metal. Similarly preservative wax can be used, gum dammar dissolved in xylene or bee's wax in spirit etc. The protective surface coating must be selected with a view to the kind and function of the object under treatment, and attention must be paid that it should be possible to remove it easily and without damaging the object at a future date.

Restoration involves dealing with damaged objects. Broken or damaged parts can be soldered, brazed or glued, according to circumstances. The points of contact of the pieces to be brazed show on the surface of the object as a light strip which can be covered either with paint or metal powder, possibly patination. Epoxide resin is now mostly used to glue metal, which

187 Inkwell of sheet brass. Central Europe, *c.* mid 19th century. Height 12.5 cm. Museum of the City of Prague.

188   Brass barber's bowl with indentation. Such bowls were used for shaving and were hung up by the ring. Central Europe, probably mid 19th century. Diameter 22 cm. Museum of the City of Prague.

can be purchased in the shops under a variety of brand names. Before these modern glues appeared, it was quite difficult to find a suitable glue for metal. This can be shown on some old recipes: 10 parts of finely floated whiting is mixed with 8 parts of casein and 10 parts of slaked lime. This mixture is diluted with water to the required density. For glue that resists boiling water and heat the following were needed: 1 kg powder clay, 80 g finest wood shavings, 40 g manganese ore, 20 g kitchen salt and 20 g borax. All was mixed together with water according to need. The resulting bonding agent had to be applied immediately.

Once glued together the object was to be slowly heated and then left to cool.

The majority of objects will not need such complicated treatment. Today the care of copper, brass and bronze involves no more than a good wash in soapy water or normal detergent solution. If the dirt is more persistent, a metal cleaner can be used, but such a cleaner should never contain sand as it might scratch the surface. After each cleaning, the object should be thoroughly rinsed in clean water, dried and polished with dry cloth. In more difficult cases, especially in the case of objects with patina, you should turn to a good and experienced specialist.

Acanthus

Arabesque

Auricle

Festoon

Mauresque

Glossary

Acanthus (Greek). Genus of plants having large spiny leaves; the conventionalized and decorative representation of these leaves became a popular motif of Greek and Roman art. The acanthus can be found in all styles of European art.

Aeruge nobilis *see* patina.

Aes grave (Latin for: heavy copper). The oldest Roman coin probably issued from 289 B.C., cast of copper. The basic unit was the **as,** which weighed 1 lb., i.e. 327 g, in the oldest period 273 g.

Aes rude (Latin for: raw copper). The oldest Roman legal tender. These were pieces of copper that had to be weighed every time and the value of the traded commodities was converted to these. They are assumed to have been in use from the first millennium B.C. to the third century B.C.

Aes signatum (Latin for: coined copper). Roman legal tender that took the place of the **aes rude.** These were pieces of copper of a definite wight marked with a picture of a ram, an eagle, a horse, etc. They were in use from the end of the fourth to the early third century B.C.

Arabesque. A type of ornament most often composed of acanthus tendrils laid out symmetrically along a vertical or horizontal axis. Sometimes the arabesque is filled with figural motifs. The arabesque arose on the basis of ancient patterns and was used widely in the Renaissance, in Neo-Classical art, Empire and the pseudo-Renaissance styles of the nineteenth century where it appears on infills, on friezes, etc.

Astragal. A narrow horizontal ornamental feature, most often in the shape of an eliptical or globular string of beads, connected by smaller links.

Auricle ornament. A type of Early Baroque ornament of northern origin. It was popular in toreutics and in carving and working metal in the hot state.

Bath bronze. Bronze with about 6 % of tin for casting small art works.

Cable ornament. A type of flat geometrical ornament composed of regular twists. Used widely to fill an area in strips. The cable motif was known in the Near East in the third mil-lennium B.C. and became typical of the early art of the Germanic tribes and in the early Middle Ages in Europe.

Calamine (hemimorphite). A hydrous zinc silicate, a rhomboidal colourless to yellow, brown, green or blue ore. Zinc ore. Used as crushed ore, known as calamine or lapis calaminaris until the eighteenth century when methods of distilling pure mineral zinc were discovered.

Chrysocal (chrysochalk). A soft alloy of golden colour, also called gilt bronze, used for art work and decorations. Its composition is not fixed but is usually based on above 90% copper with additions of lead, zinc or tin.

Festoon. A decorative feature consisting of a length of flowers, leaves or fruits linked together. Sometimes intertwined with a ribbon. It appears as such or in the form of garlands. Frequently found in ornamentation in Antiquity, the Renaissance, Baroque and Neo-Classical art.

Garland. Ornamental feature in the form of a wreath or festoon or rope of flowers, leaves and vines.

Girandole. A branched candlestick to be hung on the wall or set on a flat surface.

Grotesque. A type of ornament made up of a fantastic combination of fine vines with fruits, flowers, trophies, figures of animals, vases, etc. The grotesque was highly popular in the Renaissance, which adopted it from the art of Antiquity.

Incrustation. Inlaying the surface of an object with material of a different colour. Filling grooves in metal with another metal. Inlaying wood with another wood, with ivory or tortoiseshell is known as intarsia. Inlaid work of wood interspersed with metal, stones or ivory is called marquetry.

Japonsery. Exotic fashion of Japanese influences in the Late Baroque period simultaneous with the impact of Chinese art. Especially characteristic of the end of the nineteenth century, in the Art Nouveau period, in certain fields of the applied arts and in decorations.

Marquetry *see* incrustation.

Mauresque. A type of ornament composed of symmetrically laid out fine vines strongly stylized in the flat. Derived from Islamic art.

Meander

Palmette

Strip ornament

Astragal

Meander. A type of ornament of ancient art named after the river Meander in Asia Minor proverbial for its windings. The ornament forms an interlocking geometric line or spiral. It was highly popular at the time of Neo-Classical and Empire art.

Palmette. A stylized ornament resembling a palm leaf, derived from the Orient and elaborated in Antiquity by Greece and Rome. It appeared in numerous variations until the nineteenth century.

Paktong. An alloy originally imported from China based on copper, nickel and zinc.

Patina. A green to dark brown rust that covers the surface of copper (verdigris) or bronze through chemical influences of the atmosphere. Patina is a sign of the age of an object unless it is artificially created. The Roman poet Horace called patina of Greek bronzes 'aerugo nobilis'. Wild patina, known as rogna, is a corrosive coating resulting from chlorides on copper, basically oxichloride of copper.

Pinecone. Ornamental feature in the shape of a stylized pinecone, derived from the ornamental system of Antiquity. It was popular in the Renaissance and was used in the Baroque period as an end motif.

Platinum bronze. An alloy of nickel and tin with a small addition of platinum, which can be highly polished and retains this polish over a long period even in an adverse setting. It is used for cutlery at a composition of 90% nickel, 9% tin and 1% platinum.

Plista see verdigris.

Pumice. Spongy or cellular obsidian, a mineral of volcanic origin used as abrasive and polishing material for metal, also paper and wood. Nowadays pumice is artificially produced.

Rauschgold. German name for material used to make theatrical jewelry and mock gold. Basically very thin brass foil.

Rogna see patina.

Scroll. Early Baroque ornament of Italian origin with a massive cartouche and bizarre twists as its characteristic features, its ends twisted along the edges.

Strip ornament. Ornamental system of Early Baroque where the vines are replaced by little frames, grilles and intertwined narrow strips. Later lambrequins, fans and palmettes were added to this and, in the end, it was replaced by rocaille.

Tripel. Yellow to brownish coloured slate used for polishing metal, precious stones and glass. The name derives from the town of Tripolis in Lebanon.

Verdigris. This term is used to describe products of corrosion of copper after exposure to carbon dioxide. It has a similar composition to malachite and azurite. The effect of chlorine gives rise to oxide chlorine of copper, the minerals atakamite and nantokite.

Note

Trade Names. A variety of trade names have been given to brass alloys based on the amount of zinc and copper they contain. For example, Bath metal, Halbgold, Hamilton metal, Mannheim gold, Monel metal, Mosaic gold, New gold, Oreide, Pinchbeck, Potin, Simili-or and Sterrometal. Under 10% of zinc gives brass a copper colour, above 67% of zinc and it is of a very pale colour. The same ratio of copper to zinc gives the brass a yellow-red colour.

Pinecone

Tendrils

Scroll ornament

Bibliography

Bakurdzhiev, G., *Kovana med* (Forged Metal), Sofia 1957

Baur, V., *Kerzenleuchter aus Metall. Geschichte, Form und Technik*, Munich 1977

Blažíček, O. J., et alia, *Slovník památkové péče* (Dictionary of Care for Ancient Monuments), Prague 1962

Bloch, P., 'Siebenarmige Leuchter in christlichen Kirchen', *Wallraf—Richartz Jahrbuch* 23, 1961

Bos, E. G. G., *Vijf eeuwen koper en brons*, Amsterdam 1973

Bouchard, P. E., *La Dinanderie d'Art*, Brussels 1952

Brünning, A., *Thürgriffe und Brunnenmasken*, Berlin 1900

Collon-Gaevert, S., *Art mosan dans la vallée de la Meuse*, Brussels 1962

Dexel, W., *Das Hausgerät Mitteleuropas. Wesen und Wandel der Formen in zwei Jahrtausenden*, Brunswick-Berlin 1962

Diviš, J., 'Copper, Bronze and Brass', *Colour Encyclopaedia of Antiques*, Prague-London 1980, 1982, pp. 198-231

Encyklopedie antiky (Encyclopaedia of Antiquity), Prague 1973

Erikson, S., *Mässing. Svenska Manufakturer och Konsthandverksprodukter under 400 ar*, Stockholm 1943

Falke, O. von — Meyer, E., *Bronzegeräte des Mittelalters*, Berlin 1935

Faltermeier, K. J., 'Moderne Bronzerestaurierung', *Präparator* 16, 1970, No. 1/2, pp. 33—37

Filip, J., *Keltská civilizace a její dědictví* (Celtic Civilisation and its Heritage), Prague 1959

Fränzel, H., 'Was uns alte kupferne Geräte zu sagen haben', *Bildende Kunst*, 1966, No. 5, pp. 261—263

Gentle, R. — Feild, R., *English Domestic Brass 1680—1810*, New York 1975

Goldschmidt, A., *Die deutschen Bronzetüren des frühen Mittelalters*, Marburg 1926

Hansen, H. J., *Kunstgeschichte des Backwerks*, Oldenburg and Hamburg 1968

Hartmann, C., 'Handbuch der Metallgiesserei', *Neuer Schauplatz der Künste und Handwerke*, Vol. 103, Weimar 1840

Hesseling, E., *Appliques en bronze dans les styles Louis XIV et Louis XV*, Paris 1911

Hlubuček, K., *Poslední mědikovecké dílny* (The Last Coppersmiths' Workshops), Prague (no date)

Holmquist, K., *19th Century Brass*, Stockholm 1967

Jantzen, U., *Bronzewerkstätten in Grossgriechenland und Sizilien*, 1938 (town of issue not given)

Jantzen, U., *Griechische Greifenkessel*, Berlin 1955

Jedrzejewska, H., 'The Conservation of Ancient Bronzes', *Studies in Conservation* 9, 1964, No. 1, pp. 23—31

Kirnbauer, F. — Steiskal-Paur, R., 'Herrengrunder Kupfergegenstände', *Loebner Grüne Hefte*, Part 41, Vienna 1959

Kirnbauer, F. — Steiskal-Paur, R., *Iserlohner Dosen*, Vienna 1969

Lamb, W., *Greek and Roman Bronzes*, London 1929

Lexikon der Kunst, Vols 1—5, Leipzig 1968—78

Lockner, H. P., 'Oft kopiert und nie erreicht. Nachahmungen, Abformungen, Fälschungen von Beckenschlägerschüsseln der Zeit zwischen 1450 und 1600', *Kunst und Antiquitäten*, 1977, Part 4, pp. 37—41

Lockner, H. P., 'In der Fälscherwerkstatt. Auf den Spuren der Nachahmer von Beckenschlägerschüsseln', *Kunst und Antiquitäten*, 1978, Part 2, pp. 25—29

Lockner, H. P., *Messing 15.—17. Jahrhundert*, Munich 1982

Lovag, Z., *Mittelalterliche Bronzekunst in Ungarn*, Budapest 1979

Mathar, L. — Voigt, A., *Über die Entstehung der Metallindustrie im Bereich der Erzvorkommen zwischen Dinant und Stolberg*, Lammersdorf 1969

Mende, U., 'Kupfer-, Bronze- und Messingarbeiten', *Keysers Kunst- und Antiquitätenbuch*, Vol. 3, Munich 1967, pp. 293—386

Mende, U., 'Nürnberger Aquamalien und verwandte Gussarbeiten um 1400', *Anzeiger des Germanischen Nationalmuseums*, 1974, pp. 8—25

Mende, U., *Die Türzieher des Mittelalters*, Berlin 1981

Meyer, E., *Bronzen und Islam. Vorbilder;*

Festschrift für E. Kühnel, Berlin 1959

Meyer, E., *Mittelalterliche Bronzen*, Hamburg 1960

Morant, H. de, *Histoire des arts décoratifs des origines à nos jours*, Paris 1970

Pettorelli, A., *Il bronzo e il rame nell'arte decorativa italiana*, Milan 1930

Renaud, J. G. N., *Oude ambachts kunst*, Amsterdam 1943

Rhein und Maas: Kunst und Kultur 800—1400, Vols I—II, Cologne 1972/3

Savage, G., *A Concise History of Bronze*, London 1968

Schottmüller, F., *Bronze-Statuetten und Geräte*, Berlin 1918

Sieveking, J., *Antike Metallgeräte*, Munich 1925

Springer, P., *Kreuzfüsse. Ikonographie und Typologie eines hochmittelalterlichen Gerätes*, Berlin 1981

Steiskal-Paur, R., 'Noch einmal: Iserlohner Dosen', *Kunst und Antiquitäten*, 1979, No. 1, pp. 39—41

Stengl, W., Nürnberger Messinggerät', *Kunst und Kunsthandwerk* 21, 1918, pp. 213—265

Svoboda, B. — Conšev, D., 'Neue Denkmäler antiker Toreutik', *Monumenta archeologica*, Vol. 4, Prague 1956

Swarzenski, G., *Mittelalterliches Bronzegerät*, Berlin 1900

Tavenor-Percy, J., *Dinandery. A History and Description of Medieval Art Work in Copper, Brass and Bronze*, London 1910

Verster, A. J. G., *Bronze*, Hanover 1966

Vlachovič, J., 'Španiodolinské poháre' (Špania Dolina Goblets), *Zborník Slovenského národného múzea* (Journal of the Slovak National Museum) LXII, 1968, P. 203 ff.

Volavka, V., *Jak vzniká socha* (How a Statue Comes into Being), Prague 1956

Weitzmann-Fiedler, J., 'Romanische Bronzeschalen mit mythologischen Darstellungen', *Zeitschrift für Kunstwissenschaft* X, 1956; XI, 1957

Weitzmann-Fiedler, J., *Romanische gravierte Bronzeschalen*, Berlin 1981

Wentzel, H., 'Bettwärmer', *Reallexikon zur deutschen Kunstgeschichte*, Vol. 2, Stuttgart 1948, pp. 448—452

Werner, O., 'Analysen mittelalterlichen Bronze und Messinge I', *Archäologie und Naturwissenschaften* I, 1977, pp. 144—220

Wills, G., *Collecting Copper and Brass*, London 1962

Wills, G., *The Book of Copper and Brass*, London 1968

Wiswe, M., *Hausrat aus Kupfer und Messing*, Munich 1979

Witter, W., *Die Kenntnis von Kupfer und Bronze in der alten Welt*, Leipzig 1938

Wühr, H., *Wohnkunst und Hausrat einst und jetzt*, Darmstadt 1954

'Základy muzejní konzervace' (Elements of Museum conservation), *Muzeografické učební texty I* (Museographic Textbook), Brno 1970

List of Photographs

1 The Khasemhemwy copper vessel with a riveted double spout. Egypt, 2nd Dynasty. University of Pennsylvania, Philadelphia.

2 Bronze weight in the shape of a reclining lion from the period 530—380 B.C. Found at Susa, Iran. Musée National du Louvre, Paris.

3 Two-part stone mould for casting bronze needles. Knovíz Culture, 12th—7th century. Found near the village of Zvoliněves in Bohemia. Length of the larger part 15.5 cm. National Museum, Prague.

4 One half of a stone mould for casting bronze rings. Knovíz Culture, 12th—7th century B.C. Found near the village of Zvoliněves in Bohemia. Length 11 cm. National Museum, Prague.

5 A hoard of bronze daggers with decorated blades. Únětice Culture, 19th—15th century. Found near the village of Horoměřice in Bohemia. National Museum, Prague.

6 Bronze cult wagonette. Milaveč Culture, 13th—10th century B.C. Found near the village of Milaveč in Bohemia. Height of cauldron 25 cm, length of wagonette 30 cm. National Museum, Prague.

7 Bronze jug with spout. Etruscan export to Central Europe, 5th century B.C. Found near the village of Hradiště in Bohemia. Height 23 cm. National Museum, Prague.

8 Bronze pail with handle decorated with cast figures. Central Italian export to Central Europe, end of 1st century B.C. Found near the village of Dobřichov in Bohemia. National Museum, Prague.

9 Two bronze tripods. Italy, 1st century A.D. Height 20.3 and 17.3 cm. Museum of Decorative Arts, Prague.

10 Two bronze reliquary crosses of the type of crosses from the Holy Land. 11th century. Found in Prague. Height 6 and 8.5 cm. Museum of the City of Prague.

11 Two dishes of hammered copper decorated with engraved part-figures of angels. Maas region, 12th century. Diameter 23.5 and 27 cm. National Museum, Prague.

12 Two bronze censers. Bohemia, 13th century. Height 17.5 and 12.5 cm. National Museum, Prague.

13 Bronze cup found near the village of Libkovice in Bohemia. Silesian-Plátenice Culture, first half of 1st millennium B.C. Height 6.2 cm. National Museum, Prague.

14 Two bronze pitchers decorated with coral incrustation, found at Basse-Yutze near Metz in France. La Tène period. British Museum, London.

15 Ficoroni Cist found at Praeneste in Italy. End of 4th century B.C. Height 53 cm. Museo Nazionale di Villa Giulia, Rome.

16 Bronze scales found at Pompeii. Photo Fabrizio Parisio, Naples.

17 Bronze oil lamp found at Herculaneum. Photo Fabrizio Parisio, Naples.

18 Bronze stand for heating device found at Pompeii. Photo Fabrizio Parisio, Naples.

19 Ancient oil lamp decorated with a relief of a jumping stag. Length 13 cm. Museum of Decorative Arts, Prague.

20 Bronze oil lamp in the shape of a sailing boat symbolizing the Church. Italy, 4th century. Photo Soprintendenza Archaeologica per la Toscana, Florence.

21 Bronze grille in Charlemagne chapel in Aachen cathedral. Germany, early 9th century. Photo Ann Münchow, Aachen.

22 Bronze aquamanile from Hradec Králové, Bohemia. Lower Saxony, second half of 13th century. Height 26.5 cm. National Museum, Prague.

23   Detail of the handle of the aquamanile from Hradec Králové.

24   Gothic brass candlestick. Kutná Hora, Bohemia. Height 17.5 cm. Museum of Decorative Arts, Prague.

25   Bronze table candlestick with a figural stem. Central Europe, 15th century. Height 24 cm. National Museum, Prague.

26   Bronze baptismal font with copper lid. Slovakia, 1497. Height 100 cm. Parish church at Spišské Vlachy, Slovakia.

27   Bronze baptismal font with later copper lid. Slovakia, 1549. Height 105 cm. Parish church at Spišská Nová Ves, Slovakia.

28   Two Gothic candlesticks from the church at Plzenec and at Lovčice in Bohemia. 15th century. Height 25 and 28 cm. National Museum, Prague.

29   Bronze mortar. The upper edge bears the inscription 'ave + maria + gracia + plena + dominus'. The outer side of the mortar has the letter 'W' below a crown and the year 1490. Bohemia. Height 23 cm. Museum of Decorative Arts, Prague.

30   Bronze aquamanile found not far from a ruined medieval church in the village of Veľká Čalomija. Slovakia, early 13th century. Height 22.5 cm. Central Slovakian Museum, Banská Bystrica.

31   Two brass aquamaniles in the shape of lions. Lower Saxony, second half of 13th century. Height of the larger artifact 20 cm. Museum of Decorative Arts, Prague.

32   The Gloucester candlestick, Cast in rare copper, silver, zinc, lead and tin alloys in three parts (foot, stem and drip-tray), which are linked by an iron rod. One of the inscription reveals the origin of the candlestick. England, 12th century. Height 58.4 cm. Victoria and Albert Museum, London.

33   Bronze sanctuary ring on the door of the St Wenceslas Chapel in St Vitus' Cathedral in Prague. Alleged to have been originally on the door of the church in Stará Boleslav where Wenceslas was assassinated. Bohemia (?), second half of 12th century. Diameter of circular plate 51 cm. Photo A. Paul, Prague.

34   Hansa dish with relief bust of the Ottonian Emperor on the crossing of the two ornamental strips with relief vines. Magdeburg (?), 12th century. Diameter 30 cm. Staatliche Galerie Moritzburg, Halle.

35   Bronze censer with figural Bible scenes of the three Youths in the Fiera Oven on the lid. France, 12th century. Palais des Beaux-Arts, Lille.

36   Bronze candlestick in the shape of a man riding a lion. Maas river basin, 12th century. 32 × 25 cm. Musée des Arts Décoratifs, Paris.

37   Half-figure of St Peter on the bronze baptismal font shown in colour on photo No. 26.

38   The year 1497 on the baptismal font on colour photo No. 26. Notice the graphic form of Late Gothic numbers.

39   Bronze baptismal font standing on ten (originally twelve) figures of cattle and with five reliefs on the outside. Reiner van Huy, 1107—18. Church of St Bartholomew, Liège. Photo Bildarchiv, Marburg.

40   Bronze baptismal font. Richly decorated on the outside and the lid with reliefs of biblical scenes and the coat-of-arms of the Hildesheim bishopric and the figure of the donor Wilbernus. Hildesheim cathedral, c. 1220. Height with lid 180 cm. Largest diameter 103 cm. Bildarchiv Photo Marburg.

41   Base of the Milan candlestick in St Vitus' Cathedral in Prague. Maas region, c. mid 12th century. Height 30 cm.

42   Detail of the Milan candlestick.

43   a) Gothic candlestick on three feet in the shape of lion's paws. Central Europe, 15th century. Height 52 cm.
     b) Bronze candlestick with a profiled or knopped stem. Below the little drip tray there is a hook for the wick-cutter. Central Europe, early 16th century. Height 45.5 cm. Both candlesticks are in the collections of the Museum of the City of Prague.

44   Bronze door knocker in the shape of a lyre composed of leaves and lizards, with the bust of the Muse in the centre. Panel in the shape of a mascoroon. Italy, 16th century. Height 34 cm. Museum of Decorative Arts, Prague.

45   Detail of the door knocker on colour photo No. 44.

46   Bronze mortar. The outer side has relief figures of little angels to a design by P. Flötner. Probably work of the Prague bell-maker Brixi of Cynperk. Prague, 16th century. Height 11.5 cm. Museum of the City of Prague.

47 Detail of the ornaments on the mortar on colour photo No. 46.

48 Bronze mortar with handles in the shape of horses' heads. On the outside, relief ornaments of figures. Italy, 16th century. Height 10 cm. Museum of Decorative Arts, Prague.

49 Dish of hammered brass with a portrait of an Emperor of Antiquity in a circular medallion. Nuremberg, early 16th century. Diameter 32 cm. National Museum, Prague.

50 Detail of the ornamentation of the dish on colour photo No. 49.

51 Foot of a Romanesque candlestick found in Záběhlice, Prague. Bohemia, second half of 12th century. Height 8 cm. National Museum, Prague.

52 Bronze water jug with a loose lid. The body is decorated with relief ornaments consisting of the coat-of-arms of England and that of King Richard II (1367—1400), and the text of two proverbs. England, second half of 14th century. Height 61 cm. British Museum, London.

53 Bronze oil lamp in the shape of a boat. There are five holes around the centre of the lamp and it has an engraved vine ornament. Central Europe, 15th century. Museum of Decorative Arts, Prague.

54 Bronze baptismal font. The Latin inscription names H. Tegetmeiger and A. Eddelendes and gives the year 1492. Height 74 cm. Parish church of St Mary, Heiligenstadt.

55 Bronze baptismal font. Germany, 15th century. Height 82 cm. Former monastery church of St Martin, Heiligenstadt.

56 Late Gothic bronze mortar with four ribs. Central Europe, second half of 15th century. Height 15.5 cm. Museum of the City of Prague.

57 Two bronze taps in the shape of dolphins. Bohemia, 17th century. Length 40.5 and 32 cm. Museum of the City of Prague.

58 Bronze inkwell on three feet with relief ornaments. Italy, 16th century. Height 5.5 cm. Museum of Decorative Arts, Prague.

59 Bronze votive candlestick of the Prague guild of maltsters. The Latin dedication is dated 1532. Made by Hans Vischer of Nuremberg. Height 240 cm. St Wenceslas Chapel in St Vitus' Cathedral, Prague. Photo SÚPPOP, Prague.

60 Bronze door knocker in the shape of two figures of children, Medici emblem, mask of a satyr. Italy, 16th century. Diameter of the ring 25 cm. Museum of Decorative Arts, Prague.

61 Bronze door knocker in the shape of dolphins. The lower part has the form of a mascaroon. Italy, end of 16th century. Diameter 7.5 cm. Museum of Decorative Arts, Prague.

62 Detail of the ornaments on the mortar on colour photo No. 48.

63 Dish of hammered brass with the figure of a stag in the base. Nuremberg, 16th century. Diameter 32 cm. National Museum, Prague.

64 Copper vessel (incense-burner?) with the figure of a frog on the lid. Engraved inscription 'Folbracht 11 May 1575'. Germany (?). Height 21 cm. National Museum, Prague.

65 Bell with floral and figural decoration in relief. Engraved inscription 'S. Marcus, S. Matheus'. Italy, 16th century. Museum of Decorative Arts, Prague.

66 Two small Renaissance brass candlesticks. Central Europe, second half of 16th century. Height 11.5 cm. Museum of Decorative Arts, Prague.

67 Bronze mortar with handles in the shape of dolphins. Below the upper rim there is the inscription 'LOF - GODT - VAN - AL - A° - 1614'. Germany (?). Height 11 cm. Museum of Decorative Arts, Prague.

68 Tray on which stood Holy Communion vessels in copper with remnants of silvering. The inscription 'SUMPTIBUS P: WENCESLAY ADALBERTY ZAPEK DECANI POLNENSIS . . . 1681' is engraved on the base. Bohemia. 22.5 × 28.7 cm. National Museum, Prague.

69 Copper lavabo. Engraved inscription 'FRANTZ PAUR 1706'. Hammered decorations, tin-plated inside. Central Europe. Height 16.2 cm. National Museum, Prague.

70 Brass smoothing iron with relief decorations and the inscription 'MARIA + FRANCISCA/TERESIA + LÖWIN 1694'. Nuremberg (?). Length 18.5 cm. Museum of the City of Prague.

71 Bronze mortar. The outer side is decorated with reliefs of the Crucifixion, The Virgin and Child, angels heads and a circular medallion with an equestrian portrait of Emperor and King Ferdinand III. Bohemia or Austria,

first half of 17th century. Height 15.5 cm. Museum of the City of Prague.

72 Medallion on the mortar on colour photo No. 71. The equestrian portrait of Emperor and King Ferdinand III (1637—57). Wording: FERDINAND III D.G. RO. M.IM.

73 Copper and brass bottles with pewter caps. Central Europe, 18th century. Height of the tallest bottle 28.5 cm. Museum of the City of Prague.

74 Two typical 18th-century household articles: a pot for fish and a bed-warmer with an engraved coat-of-arms of a bishop on the lid. Height of pot 25 cm, diameter of bed-pan 28.5 cm. Museum of the City of Prague.

75 Late Renaissance brass candlestick from the turn of the 16th to 17th century. Central Europe. Height 42 cm. Museum of the City of Prague.

76 Bronze trivet with a wooden handle. The actual base composed of S-shaped ornament and conical pillars grows out of the supporting legs on which the year 1668 is engraved. The handle ends in the figure of Atlas supporting the globe. England, 1668. Length 58.4 cm. Victoria and Albert Museum, London.

77 Brass candlestick from the early 17th century. Probably German. Height 17.5 cm. Museum of Decorative Arts, Prague.

78 Bronze mortar with two handles in the form of spikes. Central Europe, 17th century. Height 9 cm. Museum of Decorative Arts, Prague.

79 Three examples of Baroque candlesticks. On the left, the candlestick with the hectagonal base and relief heads of little angels on the drip tray dates from the 17th century. In the centre the candlestick from the 18th century is decorated with twisted fluting. The candlestick on the right has a propped stem and a wide flat base. Height of the left candlestick 28.5 cm. Museum of the City of Prague.

80 Water holder made from sheet copper and engraved with flowers and the letters 'T. A. F. Anno 1705'. Height 25 cm. Pinkas Synagogue, State Jewish Museum, Prague.

81 Two flint-and-steel clocks with a lighting mechanism. The clockwork case is made of gilded brass. Brass was popular among clock-makers. The clock is signed 'Ferdinant Engelschalck/Prag' and 'Johan Maurer/Prag'. Engelschalck's workshop is recorded in Prague for the years 1705—52, Maurer's from 1725—31. The size of the clocks is almost identical, 17 × 9 × 5.5 cm. Museum of the City of Prague.

82 Dial and case with the signature of the maker of the alarm and lighting mechanism of the flint-and-steel clock in picture 81.

83 Copper pot on three iron legs with an iron handle. Hammered inscription: 'M.C.Lara 1738'. South Germany (?). Height 32.5 cm. Museum of the City of Prague.

84 Jug of sheet copper. At the front a hammered maltsters' emblem (two crossed maltsters' tools) between two walking lions. The year 1747 is hammered on the lid. Bohemia. Height 34 cm. Museum of the City of Prague.

85 Tub hammered of sheet copper. A similar emblem of the maltsters as on jug in picture No. 84 is depicted on the body of the tub. Two iron handles. Bohemia, mid 18th century. Upper diameter 30 cm. Museum of the City of Prague.

86 Copper box with lid, brass mounts, with an iron handle on the lid. Austria, 17th century. Height 27 cm. Museum of the City of Prague.

87 Copper jug with a rim for it to be set in a hole in the stove-top. Central Europe, end of 18th century. Height 35 cm. National Museum, Prague.

88 Brass candlestick with four branches for use on the Jewish Sabbath. An eagle at top centre. Eastern Europe, c. mid 18th century. Height 45.5 cm. State Jewish Museum, Prague.

89 Bronze andirons of a man and woman with cock and hen tails. Signed 'Caffieri fecit' (Jacques Caffieri). France, first half of 18th century. Musée des Arts Décoratifs, Paris.

90 a) Copper chalice with hammered and engraved decorations. It is decorated with (1) the coat-of-arms of the guild of butchers (the Bohemian lion with a hatchet in the front paws); (2) coat-of-arms of the Old Town of Prague; (3) the inscription '1700 / Johhan Kletezka / 1750'. The letters S.R.J.B.W.Z.K. are hammered along the upper rim of the cup, on the stem the letters M/J/K. Prague. Height 18.2 cm.
b) Copper chalice with S-shaped hammered ribs and an inscription around the upper edge of the cup: 'DAVID. BEN. ABR. OPPENHEIMER 1720'. Prague (?). Height 16.5 cm. Both chalices are the property of the Museum of the City of Prague.

91 Bronze holy water font with relief orna-

ments of heads of angels. Gilded. At the back the year 1758 is engraved. Austria or southern Germany. Height of back wall 22 cm. Museum of Decorative Arts, Prague.

92 Set of tobacco boxes of brass and copper sheet. These boxes with repoussé relief are marked in the decoration: 'GIESE / ISER-LOHN'. The tobacco grater is decorated with perforated ornament including the coat-of-arms of the maltsters, the letters ASS and the year 1762. The tobacco box on the right is signed 'HAMER FEC ISERLOHN'. Length 15 cm. Museum of the City of Prague and private collection, Prague.

93 Brass weights 32 lbs and 8 lbs. Nuremberg, second half of 18th century. Height of the largest weight 29.3 cm. National Museum, Prague.

94 Detail of one of the weights on colour photo No. 93.

95 View of Prague. Part of the decoration on the tobacco box on colour photo No. 92.

96 Articles of copper made at Špania Dolina, Slovakia, 17th—19th century. Museum of Decorative Arts, Prague.

97 Copper jug with the hammered figure of a lion on the lid. The year 1762 is engraved on the lid. Height 34 cm. Museum of the City of Prague.

98 Commode in the royal bedroom at Versailles. To a design by court artist S. A. Slodtz made by ebenist A. R. Gaudreau, gilt bronze decorations by Jacques Caffieri. Paris, 1739. Wallace Collection, London.

99 Foot-warmer of sheet brass, octagonal. Hammered inscription 'Nicolas Schmuck Anno 1753'. Germany. Height 9.5 cm. Museum of Decorative Arts, Prague.

100 Wine cooler in sheet copper with hammered ornament. Two iron handles. Central Europe, c. mid 18th century. Largest diameter 55 cm. Museum of the City of Prague.

101 Brass was highly suitable for the production of various instruments. The equatorial sun-dial depicted is signed 'Franciscus Merl fecit Pragae A:1735'. Height 21 cm, diameter of the round plate 17.5 cm. Museum of the City of Prague.

102 Copper jug decorated on the lower part with an S-shaped hammered ornamentation. Similar decoration is found on the lid. The spout is oblong in shape. Iron handle. Central Europe, before mid 18th century. Height in-

cluding lid 45 cm. Museum of the City of Prague.

103 Painting by an anonymous painter showing the birth of John the Baptist. It renders proof that the original function of the copper tub for cooling beverages was lost by the end of the 18th century. Private collection, Prague.

104 Andirons of gilt bronze with figures of Chinese men and women from Bellevue château. Louis XV style. Musée National du Louvre, Paris.

105 Table alarm-clock. A hexagonal case of gilded bronze mounted in silver on three shaped legs. Enamel dial. Signed 'Johann Engelschalk in Prag'. The work of J. Engelschalk is recorded in Prague for the years 1754—74. Diameter 9.5 cm. Museum of the City of Prague.

106 The writing desk of Louis XV. Work on the table was begun by the ebenist J. F. Oeben in 1760 and after his death the desk was finished by J. H. Riesener in 1769. The gilt bronze ornaments on the desk were modelled by Duplessis, cast and chased by L. Hervieu. Signed 'Riesener H.f., 1769 à l'Arsenal de Paris'. Musée National du Château de Versailles.

107 Brass lamp decorated with two relief lions holding the portrait of the Austrian Emperor Joseph II. Bohemia, c. 1785. Width 28.5 cm. State Jewish Museum, Prague.

108 Copper container in which hot embers were kept overnight in the Netherlands, where these were called 'Doovpötte'; brass lid and handle. End of 18th century. Height 34 cm. Private collection, Prague.

109 Detail of the dish on colour photo No. 96.

110 Tankard with gilded copper lid. On the lid there is a small figure of a miner. On the medallion on the vessel the inscription is engraved on a gilt background: 'Gott / lass einkehren aller orten / Gold Silber und Kupfer / sorten, zu Kremnitz Schem / nitz und Neüsohl, gera / the Gold Silber und Kupfer wohl'. On the rim: 'Gott beschere alles mild was ich führ in meinem Schild'. Špania Dolina, Slovakia, 18th century. Height with lid 14.2 cm. Museum of Decorative Arts, Prague.

111 Brass plate-warmer in the shape of a pan with wooden handles and a double base on three legs. Germany, end of 18th century. Diameter 20 cm. Museum of Decorative Arts, Prague.

232

112　Avignon clock. Cast, chased and gilded to a design by sculptor Louis Simon Boizot by Pierre Gouthière. Paris, 1771. Wallace Collection, London.

113　Copper vessel with brass spout and attachments for iron handle, which used to be hung above a washbasin. Popular in Switzerland where it was called 'Brunnenkesselchen'. Switzerland, c. 1700. Height 28 cm. Museum of the City of Prague.

114　Copper vessel for cooling beverages, with hammered decorations. Between the acanthus there are mascaroons, the maltsters coat-of-arms and the year 1743. Height 32 cm. Museum of the City of Prague.

115　Detail of the decoration on the cooler on photo No. 114.

116　Oval copper container with hammered sculpture of lions on the lid. Central Europe, 18th century. 15.5×11×10.5 cm. National Museum, Prague.

117　Copper bottle with a screw top. The coat-of-arms of the Prague family of Wunschwitz and the letter 'W' below a crown on the outside. The pewter top has the mark of the pewterer and the year 1732. Prague. Height 29 cm. Museum of the City of Prague.

118　Copper tripod with an iron handle for use on an open fire. Central Europe, 18th century. Height excluding the handle 30.5 cm. Private collection, Prague.

119　Table heater of copper, with a wooden handle, which used charcoal. Central Europe, end of 18th century. Largest diameter 18.5 cm. Museum of the City of Prague.

120　A set of two candlesticks and a clock. The clock-dial has the words: 'V^{or} PAILLARD / F$_t$ DE BRONZES / PARIS'. The sculpture on the clock is signed 'CLODION / Michal Claude, 1738—1814'. France, end of 18th century. Sylva-Taroucca Palace, Prague.

121　Jewel-box of gilded brass. The lid and sides of the box are decorated with engraved figures of the personified virtues. On the lid: FIDES (Faith) and IUSTICIA (Justice). On the front CHARITAS (Charity) and PRUDENTIA (Prudence). On the back: FORTIDVTO (Fortitude) and a figure without an inscription, but to judge by the attributes, it is TEMPERATIA (Temperance). On the right side there is the figure of SPES (Hope) and on the left PACIENCIA (Patience). Austria or southern Germany, least quarter of 19th century. Width 7.2 cm, depth 4.7 cm, height 4.4 cm. Private collection, Prague.

122　Hanukkah lamp also used on Saturdays. The back is formed of two stags turned towards the middle, the sides are in the shape of lions. Brass. Poland, c. 1800. Height 31 cm. State Jewish Museum, Prague.

123　Inkwell in the Louis XVI style. Three glass containers adorned with brass mounts set in a black polished wooden panel on four brass feet. The wooden panel is decorated with six brass mounts in the shape of lyres. All the brass parts are gilded. France, end of 18th century. Length 21.3 cm, width 14 cm, height 13 cm. Museum of Decorative Arts, Prague.

124　Table alarm-clock. The circular case is of gilded bronze on four legs in the shape of paws. Signed 'Johann Müller in Prag'. C. 1800. Height 14 cm. Museum of the City of Prague.

125　Two bronze gilt candlesticks with figures of amorettes climbing a flagstaff. After Louis Léopold Boilly in the style of the First Empire. France, early 19th century. Height 62 cm. Musée Marmottan, Paris.

126　Elm table decorated with figures of carryatids made of gilt bronze. The other decorations are of the same gilt bronze. The bronze parts and mounts are the work of P.-Ph. Thomire. Signed 'Jacob D. Desmalter rue meslée'. Paris, before 1813. Height 92 cm. Length 140 cm. Depth 73 cm. Grand Trianon, Versailles, Paris.

127　Smoothing irons from the first half of the 19th century. The iron at the back uses charcoal, the others have a metal core. Central Europe. Museum of the City of Prague.

128　Detail of the smoothing iron in picture No. 127 on the left.

129　Two typical articles of kitchenware from the first half of the 19th century. Copper salt-box to be hung on the wall, adorned with engraving and the date 1815, and brass mortar from roughly the same date. Central Europe. Height of salt-box with back 26 cm. Museum of Decorative Arts, Prague.

130　Two brass lamps of the Florentine type with three oil burners. A wick-cutter on a chain is attached to each lamp as well as damper tweezers. Southern Europe, c. 1800. Height 44.5 and 44 cm. State Jewish Museum, Prague.

131　Brass Empire candlestick with a square base decorated with astragal ornaments. Bohemia, c. 1820. Height 21 cm. Museum of the City of Prague.

132 Round lamp of sheet brass with an oil burner. Germany (?), *c.* mid 19th century. Height 11.5 cm. Museum of the City of Prague.

133 Hanukkah lamp which also served as a Saturday candlestick. The back part is an architectural form from Eastern Europe. Poland (?), first half of 19th century. State Jewish Museum, Prague.

134 Detail of the Hanukkah lamp in picture No. 133.

135 Typical brass candlesticks from the late 19th century. The popularity of candlesticks of this shape lasted into the early 20th century. Central Europe. Height 20 and 21 cm. Museum of the City of Prague.

136 Bronze inkwell. Gilded and black painted. France, first half of 19th century. Height 19.5 cm. Private collection, Prague.

137 Two Empire brass candlesticks with stems in the shape of caryatids. Austria (?), first quarter of 19th century. Height 21 cm. Museum of the City of Prague.

138 Two sugar-bowls of sheet brass. Central Europe, before mid 19th century. Height of the larger bowl 8.5 cm. Museum of the City of Prague.

139 Two typical jugs of the early 19th century. Copper plate. Central Europe. Height of the larger jug 39 cm. Museum of the City of Prague.

140 Empire bronze candlestick combined with a glass sculpture of a dolphin. Probably Bohemia, *c.* 1820. Height 26.5 cm. Museum of Decorative Arts, Prague.

141 Set of baking tins for cakes and puddings. Central Europe, 19th century. Diameter of the cake tin 26.5 cm. Museum of the City of Prague.

142 Brass writing set. Gilded and black patinated. Made by the Prague craftsman Isák. Prague, early 19th century. Museum of the City of Prague.

143 Altar candlestick in the Neo-Renaissance style. Designed by B. Wachsman, 1863. Height 42 cm. Church of SS Cyril and Methodius, Prague.

144 Hammered water container in copper plate. Brass tap. Moravia, *c.* 1880. Height 26.5 cm. State Jewish Museum, Prague.

145 Copper candlestick with an adjustable holder for the candle known as a 'patent' holder in use by the 18th century. Central Europe, *c.* mid 19th century. Height 18.5 cm. Museum of the City of Prague.

146 Writing desk of unpolished and unstained oak, decorated with copper mounts. To a design by C. F. A. Voysey. England, 1896. Victoria and Albert Museum, London.

147 Art Nouveau copper vessel with two handles. Probably Germany, *c.* 1900. Height 25 cm. Museum of Decorative Arts, Prague.

148 Art Nouveau copper 'samovar'. Austria, *c.* 1903. Height 33.5 cm. Museum of Decorative Arts, Prague.

149 Two stems of electric lamps of sheet brass. Bohemia, after 1900. Height 28 cm. State Jewish Museum, Prague.

150 Hanukkah brass candlestick adorned with the relief figure of a lion. Prague, early 20th century. (Clearly inspired by an older pattern.) Height 14 cm. State Jewish Museum, Prague.

151 Brass emblem decorating the guild treasury of the Brno brassmakers, showing the tools of their trade and the inscription 'Johann Schneider'. Early 19th century. Height 12.5 cm. Museum of the City of Brno.

152 Liturgical vessel for incense made of sheet brass. In the shape of a boat with legs in the shape of dolphins. Example of Baroque toreutics. Bohemia, 18th century. Height 15.5 cm. Museum of the City of Prague.

153 Brass miner's lamp. The monogram I T S is engraved on the handle with two crossed miners' hammers and the year 1763. Example of minor metal-casting work. Bohemia. Height of holder excluding handle 3.5 cm. Museum of Decorative Arts, Prague.

154 Bronze vessel on three legs with a handle to be hung over the fire. Relief decorations with the monogram of Christ and the Virgin Mary and the year 1750. Example of more exacting metal-casting. Austria or southern Germany. Height excluding handle 34 cm. Museum of Decorative Arts, Prague.

155 Jacques Caffieri: Design for the ornamentation of the baldaquin or pall of the Paris guild of braziers. Ink drawing on paper. Signed 'Invanté et dessiné par Jacques Caffieri 1715'. 67×49 cm. Musée de Tessé, Le Mans.

156 Brass candlestick in Neo-Gothic style. Central Europe, after 1850. Height 61.8 cm. Museum of Decorative Arts, Prague.

157   Art Nouveau copper wine cooler. Jan Eisenloeffel (?), Netherlands (?), after 1900. Height 22.5 cm. Museum of Decorative Arts, Prague.

158   Copper teapot decorated with niello and brass mounts. Austria (?), *c.* 1900. Height 22.5 cm. Museum of Decorative Arts, Prague.

159   Box of hammered brass sheet. Stamped in the base: 'WIENER/WERK/STATTE' and the signature of the craftsman Josef Holi. Vienna, *c.* 1920. Height 12 cm. Museum of Decorative Arts, Prague.

160   Two boxes of zinc and copper plate. Signed 'ARTĚL PRAHA'. Designed by V. Hofman. Prague, 1918. Height 10.5 cm. Museum of Decorative Arts, Prague.

161   Table lamp of sheet brass. Designed by J. Gočár. Prague, first quarter of 20th century. Height 28.5 cm. Museum of Decorative Arts, Prague.

162   Altar candlestick of brass adorned with polished semi-precious stones. Designed by J. Plečnik. Prague, 1932. Height 48 cm. Church of the Holy Heart of the Lord, Prague.

163   Example of the chloride corrosion on a bronze object. The metal core of the mortar is almost completely broken down by corrosion. This mortar was excavated in Prague in 1912 close to a spot where saltpetre was produced in the past. Height of the torso 18.5 cm.

164   Seal of the Brno guild of brass-makers. The frieze along the edge holds the inscription 'SIG DER EHRBA UN HAND DER GELBGISS ZU BRINN 1779'. Diameter 4 cm. Archives of the City of Brno.

165   Shop sign of brazier G. Carlson. Oil on metal. Sweden, *c.* 1800. 73×63 cm. Nordiska Museet, Stockholm.

166   Forged door-lock of gilded bronze with the typical relief decorations of the late 18th century. Cental Europe. Length 18 cm. Museum of Decorative Arts, Prague.

167   Examples of mounts from the end of the 18th century, made almost in series either by casting brass or pressing brass sheet. Central Europe. Height *c.* 7 cm. Museum of Decorative Arts, Prague.

168   Two gilded brass knobs as often found on furniture drawers at the turn of the 18th to 19th century. Central Europe. Largest diameter 6.5 cm. Museum of Decorative Arts, Prague.

169   Horse harness decoration in the shape of a comb with relief figures at the top. Cast brass. Probably Nuremberg, before mid 19th century. Museum of Decorative Arts, Prague.

170   Wicker furnace. Reproduction from the book by V. Biringuccio *De la pirotechnia libri X* (first edition 1540).

171   Plan of a circular furnace. Reproduced from the book by V. Biringuccio *De la pirotechnia libri X* (first edition 1540).

172   Set of brass weights, known as the Vienna pound (i.e. 0.56 kg): 1/2 lb, 1 lb, and 2 lbs. Prague, before 1871. Height of the 1/2 lb weight 5 cm. Museum of the City of Prague.

173   Seal of the Brno guild of copper-makers. The inscription on the frieze around the edge reads 'SIGIL DES LOBLICHEN HANTWERCK D KUPFERSCHMIE IN D KONIGSDAT PRIN 1664'. Diameter 4.2 cm. Archives of the City of Brno.

174   Brass Saturday candlestick in the shape of a double-headed eagle. The oval breastplate of the eagle has a star of David engraved into it. Poland, first half of 19th century. Height 40.5 cm. State Jewish Museum, Prague.

175   Wall coat-of-arms of coppersmith J. S. Müller. Fresco on the wall of a house at Nördlingen, 1769. 140×190 cm. Photo Bayer. Landesamt für Denkmalpflege, Munich.

176   Set of children's cups and plates from the first half of the 19th century. These toys were exact copies of contemporary household utensils. Central Europe. Height of pot 2.5 cm. National Museum, Prague.

177   Copper pot with spout, lid and two handles. Example of good quality work of a coppersmith around the mid 19th century. Bohemia. Height excluding lid 23 cm. Museum of the City of Prague.

178   Detail showing how the iron handle was attached to a copper pot. Second half of 18th century.

179   Wick snuffers were a typical produce of brass-makers. These three examples were made by Bohemian or Prague brassmakers at the end of the 18th and in the early 19th century. Length of the smallest 6.5 cm. Museum of the City of Prague.

180   Jug of copper plate adorned with hammered floral decoration. Central Europe, first half of 18th century. Height 41.5 cm. Museum of the City of Prague.

181 Copper barrel with a hammered scene of a coppersmith's workshop. Dated 1899. Property of the Prague Community of Coppersmiths. Height 11.5 cm. Museum of the City of Prague.

182 Holy water font of copper plate. Such fonts, often also made of pewter, were usually to be found in households. Bohemia, second half of 18th century. Height 15.5 cm. Private collection, Prague.

183 Coffee grinder of sheet brass. Central Europe, c. mid 19th century. Height 23 cm. Museum of the City of Prague.

184 Brass rulers. The twopartite one is the Vienna foot, divided on one side into 12 inches and 96 lines along the other. The year 1695 is punched on the ridge. The three-partite ruler is a yard-stick from the end of the 18th century. Bohemia or Austria. Museum of the City of Prague.

185 Two coffee machines of sheet brass. Central Europe, first half of 19th century. Height 42 cm. Museum of the City of Prague.

186 Brass spice-box. The tin-covered interior is divided into several compartments. Central Europe, c. mid 19th century. 15.5×10.5×7 cm. Museum of the City of Prague.

187 Inkwell of sheet brass. Central Europe, c. mid 19th century. Height 12.5 cm. Museum of the City of Prague.

188 Brass barber's bowl with indentation. Such bowls were used for shaving and were hung up by the ring. Central Europe, probably mid 19th century. Diameter 22 cm. Museum of the City of Prague.

Index

Roman numbers indicate pages. Numbers in italics are those of the illustrations.